Soup for Academic Leaders

Acquire Teaching Tools to Achieve Your Academic Leadership Success

M.S. Rao

ATLANTIC

PUBLISHERS & DISTRIBUTORS (P) LTD

Published by
ATLANTIC
PUBLISHERS & DISTRIBUTORS (P) LTD
7/22, Ansari Road, Darya Ganj,
New Delhi-110002
Phones : +91-11-40775252, 23273880, 23275880, 23280451
Fax : +91-11-23285873
Web : www.atlanticbooks.com
E-mail : orders@atlanticbooks.com

Branch Office
5, Nallathambi Street, Wallajah Road,
Chennai-600002
Phones : +91-44-64611085, 32413319
E-mail : chennai@atlanticbooks.com

Printed in India at Nice Printing Press, A-33/3A, Site-IV,
Industrial Area, Sahibabad, Ghaziabad, U.P.

Dedication

To my grandfather—Meka Narasimha Swamy, and grandmother—Meka Satyanarayanamma.

To educators who aspire to make a difference in the lives of students with their passion, knowledge, and leadership.

To students who are the future leaders on whose shoulders the future of the nation depends.

Foreword

When International Leadership Guru, Professor M.S. Rao requested me to write a foreword for his new book, *Soup for Academic Leaders: Acquire Teaching Tools to Achieve Your Academic Leadership Success*, it was a true honor. He has the endorsements of some of the world's greatest leadership professionals, which shows his credentials as an international leadership author, expert, and guru. He has authored 15 books on leadership, which indicates his passion for leadership and writing, and above all, his passion to make a difference in the lives of others.

Professor M.S. Rao hails from academic background, with an interest in leadership. He has authored this book to honor teachers who are the backbone of the society. He blended his both passions—academics and leadership, and highlighted on academic leadership as teachers are the true leaders in the society who create leaders in other professions.

Leadership starts with education, but also from within, and is demonstrated in the way we act and react. It starts with our attitude, the foundation of all successful people. It is then reflected in our daily behaviors—our effective and ineffective habits.

As a leader, in any field, we must demonstrate the appropriate behaviors that we want others to follow. It is as simple as "Monkey See, Monkey Do!" You are the Monkey and your followers will do as they see you do. Hence, there is a need to always demonstrate appropriate behaviors, particularly in the field of education.

As an academic leader, answer the following questions for yourself:

- Are you demonstrating the appropriate behaviors that you want others to follow?

- Are you sharing your knowledge with others in an educational manner—in a manner that they can share it with others too?
- Are you coaching for success and building self-esteem and confidence in others? If so, are you engaging them through self-discovery so that they take ownership?

These are only some of the questions that *Soup for Academic Leaders: Acquire Teaching Tools to Achieve Your Academic Leadership Success* will help you answer.

Professor M.S. Rao understands leadership well and has laid out a concise and efficient way of understanding the fundamentals of Academic Leadership, while providing the tools and techniques for training and teaching methodologies.

He understands the role of teachers in shaping students and the nation, as he himself has been inspired by many teachers, and wants to contribute in a positive way to the nation as well.

Besides interesting case studies, stories, anecdotes, and illustrations, the book provides a series of practical, proven, easy-to-apply ideas, and strategies that help you become a more successful academic leader. It is an inspirational book for educators, students, coaches, trainers, leaders, and learners, and especially for those who are passionate to share their knowledge with others, and aspire to excel as academic leaders.

This is your opportunity to learn and lead from the inside out and not only make a difference in your own life as an academic leader, but in the lives of others too. Step up, study this book, take control and make the difference the academic world is waiting for. Only you can make the difference.

Bob Urichuck,

Ranked #4 in the World's Top 30 Sales Gurus

International Professional Speaker, Trainer, and Author of *Disciplined for Life; You Are the Author of Your Future;* and *Up Your Bottom Line* featuring the "Buyer Focused" Velocity Selling System.

Preface

Education is the mother of leadership.—*Wendell L. Willkie*

Welcome to *Soup for Academic Leaders: Acquire Teaching Tools to Achieve Your Academic Leadership Success.* You may be wondering why I am doing a book of this genre as I basically author books on leadership. I have passion for teaching, writing and consulting. Teaching profession is a highly respected profession where teachers command respect when they teach with a true heart to make a difference in the lives of students. Hence, I have authored this book on academic leadership by including management education, success, coaching, and leadership.

This book is divided into five chapters underscoring academic leadership; management education; success; coaching; and leadership. Part I of this book preludes with praising teaching profession as it is the mother of all professions, and teachers are the true leaders who shape students as leaders. Future of students and a nation depends on the teachers and their contribution towards their teaching profession. It explains the types of teaching, characteristics of teachers, and tools and techniques of teaching. It outlines elaborately why someone should choose teaching as a career. It unveils the ways and means to excel as successful teachers. It asserts that great teachers are not born in the minds of the students, but they are born in the hearts of the students. It introduces an innovative teaching tool—Meka's Method® coined by me, to engage students effectively in the classroom to ensure effective teaching outcomes. It is a structured and methodical way of teaching where the content is delivered on a platter as per the context and situation to ensure effective teaching outcomes. It blends various ingredients such as visual, auditory, storytelling, role-plays, participation, interaction, cooperation, communication, collaboration, and contribution to ensure effective teaching takeaways among the students.

It highlights effective teaching, and unfolds the ways to motivate students. It underscores the role of a teacher who wears different hats, and explains various skills, and styles of teaching. It unveils how to provide feedback and evaluate the teaching process. It identifies that students have the breadth of knowledge in all disciplines and teachers have the depth of knowledge in a particular domain or discipline, and that marks the difference between the students and the teachers.

Discipline problems are a major concern for teachers. With the rapid changes in technology and the major influence of media on the students there are certain behavioral changes, which are at variance with the accepted standards and norms. As a result, teachers find it difficult to manage the students in the classroom. It suggests solutions to maintain classroom discipline. It describes 6 essential Cs needed for teachers. It focuses on sandwich feedback, and how to handle question-and-answer sessions in the classroom effectively. It calls upon the teachers, students, parents, and administration for effective coordination and synchronization for ensuring favorable learning environment in the classroom.

Teachers, trainers, and presenters often face difficulties in delivering presentations due to lack of adequate expertise in the usage of cue cards. Cue cards often make or break the presentations. It discusses the case study of Robert who failed to get selected as a trainer during employment interview as he did not use cue cards during presentation. It describes the merits, precautions, stages, and tips for cue cards. It dwells on types of presentations and the techniques to be used during presentation. It outlines action exercises to engage the audiences in preparation of cue cards. It asserts that cue cards are clue cards and play a crucial role in teaching and training programs. Part I concludes that principals are the academic leaders who lead various stakeholders through their academic leadership.

Part II deals with management education by differentiating between local and global business schools. It unfolds the various challenges encountered by management educators. It explains elaborately various types of professors based on their academic, industry, research, consultancy and training backgrounds and asserts that every professor has his or her own competency. It justifies that no two professors are alike as they hail from different backgrounds. It illustrates Harvard Business School's Professor, Dr. Howard Gardner's Five Minds: disciplined mind, synthetic mind, creative mind, respectful mind, and ethical mind. It implores educators to learn from various sources including students without any false ego. It calls upon educators to become facilitators, and advises them to do continuous research to earn respect from students and to stand out as academic leaders.

It explains the importance of MBA degree and the challenges faced by students. It unfurls the aspirations and expectations of the industry, and implores students to meet the industry expectations to enhance their employability skills. It differentiates between the managers and the leaders, and describes the achievements of overseas Indians who made it big by shifting from their comfort zones to effective zones. It explains the qualities of an ideal business school student, the mode of teaching in business schools, the students' evaluation procedure, and the ways to bridge the gap between the campus and the industry. It investigates what is not taught in business schools, and how to ensure a complete management education to produce successful managers and leaders. Part II concludes with the challenges involved in pursuing PhD and PDC (Post Doctoral Course) and asserts that acquisition of doctoral degree has become a decoration for industry experts, a qualification for academicians, and a paper degree for passionate researchers in India.

Part III highlights success, and it declares that managing success is more challenging than failures. Life has become highly challenging with a lot of complexity and uncertainty. Therefore, it is essential to manage multiple channels within your mind, and take a call by blending your head, heart, and gut. It explains knowledge management, and the need to blend both business acumen and social acumen. It outlines the tools to sharpen your saw. It advises not to get dejected by setbacks but to keep moving forward as God is making you stronger and greater by unlocking your hidden potential. It calls upon to hold your hope high.

Part IV deals with coaching. It explains Dale Carnegie's six kinds of fear, and advises you to treat change as a friend rather than a foe. It explains the need for leaders to facilitate change smoothly and successfully. It profiles Marshall Goldsmith—the coaching legend, and his famous works *MOJO* and *What Got You Here Won't Get You There*. It justifies that he is a Level 5 Leader with a professional will and personal humility. It highlights Talent Conversations and emphasizes that it is an integral part of coaching and leadership development. The leaders and supervisors must have dialogue and discussion with their subordinates and handhold them to quicken their career advancement. This part concludes with a call that 'What Got You Here Will Get You There' only when you hire good coaches.

Part V begins with a message that leadership is not a hype, but a hope to face challenges squarely and resolve them successfully. It asserts that leadership is not a passing cloud for great leaders, and emphasizes that all good people may not be good leaders but all good leaders may be good people. It warns about leadership decay, and advises leaders to change and reinvent constantly with latest technological tools and techniques to remain relevant, and to succeed in this cut-throat competitive world. It explores Level 6 Leader, and mobilizes support for Nobel Prize for the disciplines of management and mathematics. It unfolds Indians' appetite for management and highlights about growing Indian management gurus globally. The book concludes with a call to face problems squarely, develop a great mindset with simplicity and humility, and see positive things in others to excel as a leader.

Leadership can be a joy, and it is always a privilege. I hope this book will inspire you to make it a priority, learn as much as you can, commit time and attention to acquire teaching tools and techniques to make a difference in the lives of students, and continue to learn and grow as an academic leader.

M.S. Rao

Acknowledgments

Writing a book is never a solo project. I am deeply indebted to many people whose expertise, wisdom, and encouragement kept me going. My wife's and children's (Ganesh Sai and Ramakrishna Sayee) encouragement and sacrifice made this book possible, and for that I am forever thankful. My wife, Padmavathy is a symbol of sacrifice and support for my books, and also is an immeasurable blessing in my life.

Several quotes, examples and anecdotes are the result of a collection from different sources. It is practically impossible to acknowledge each one of them separately. While I have tried to give credit wherever it is due, in case I have missed anything, I will give due credit in future editions if it is brought to my notice.

I thank everyone including the team of Atlantic Publishers and Distributors Pvt. Ltd. for publication of this book. I specifically thank Harjeet Singh, Publication Coordinator for his coordination in the publication of this book.

I express special thanks to all the readers who graciously took time off from their busy schedule to write to me, share their views, and offer feedback on my books. I wholeheartedly thank them for their endless support and love.

M.S. Rao

Quotes

"Education is what survives when what has been learned has been forgotten."—B.F. Skinner

"Education is the best provision for old age."—Aristotle

"Education is the most powerful weapon which you can use to change the world."—Nelson Mandela

"What sculpture is to a block of marble education is to the human soul."—Joseph Addison

"Education makes a people easy to lead but difficult to drive: easy to govern, but impossible to enslave."—Peter Brougham

"If you are planning for a year, sow rice; if you are planning for a decade, plant trees; if you are planning for a lifetime, educate people."—Chinese Proverb

"There are two kinds of teachers: the kind that fill you with so much quail shot that you can't move, and the kind that just gives you a little prod behind and you jump to the skies." — Robert Frost

"If a country is to be corruption free and become a nation of beautiful minds, I strongly feel there are three key societal members who can make a difference. They are the father, the mother and the teacher."—Abdul Kalam

"Teaching is a calling too. And I've always thought that teachers in their way are holy—angels leading their flocks out of the darkness."—Jeannette Walls, *Half Broke Horses*

"Books are the quietest and most constant of friends; they are the most accessible and wisest of counselors, and the most patient of teachers."—Charles William Eliot

"There is nothing training cannot do. Nothing is above its reach. It can turn bad morals to good; it can destroy bad principles and recreate good ones; it can lift men to angelship."—Mark Twain

"I would caution student teachers to always be flexible with kids, but not to leave them with no structure, because many times we are the only structure these kids have." —Kouzes and Posner

"This is at the heart of all good education, where the teacher asks students to think and engages them in encouraging dialogues, constantly checking for understanding and growth."—William Glasser

"It is impossible for a man to learn what he thinks he already knows."—Epictetus

"You can teach a student a lesson for a day; but if you can teach him to learn by creating curiosity, he will continue the learning process as long as he lives."—Clay P. Bedford

"Keep away from people who try to belittle your ambitions. Small people always do that, but the really great make you feel that you, too, can become great."—Mark Twain

"The first problem for all of us, men and women, is not to learn, but to unlearn."—Gloria Steinem

"Do not train children to learning by force and harshness, but direct them to it by what amuses their minds, so that you may be better able to discover with accuracy the peculiar bent of the genius of each."—Plato

"Everything that happens to you is your teacher. The secret is to learn to sit at the feet of your own life and be taught by it."—Polly Berends

Contents

PART I
Academic Leadership

1

Teachers are True Leaders

> A teacher affects eternity; he can never tell where his influence stops.—*Henry B. Adams*

Welcome to *Soup for Academic Leaders: Acquire Teaching Tools to Achieve Your Academic Leadership Success*! I authored this book to underscore the role of educators who shape the future of students, and society as a whole. I covered various aspects of education, success, coaching, and leadership with anecdotes, illustrations, and short stories to benefit readers. I have included leadership as it is close to my heart and blended both education and leadership, and highlighted academic leadership. Educators are the real leaders who lead from the front to share their knowledge with their passion by setting an example to students to shape them as successful citizens. I am excited to see that the book is in your hands now.

Teachers are True Leaders

> A good teacher is like a candle—it consumes itself to light the way for others.—*Author Unknown*

Teaching is the mother of all professions, and teachers are the true leaders. As a mark of respect to teachers, Indians celebrate Teachers Day on 5th September every year. It is the birth anniversary of Dr. S. Radhakrishnan, the former President of India, who was a great teacher and leader. According to the Hindu philosophy, next to mother and father it is the teacher who enjoys immense respect. Globally, teachers are respected because of their role to shape students and build nations.

To teach is to ignite the imagination of students. To teach is to touch the lives of others. To teach is to share knowledge with others. To teach is to enlighten others. To teach is to show the way for others. To teach is to make a difference in the lives of others. To teach is to learn twice as the teacher takes tons of pain to read, understand and create new things to share with students.

Some people think teaching is the easiest thing in the world. In fact, teaching requires too much of commitment and concentration because if a teacher speaks wrongly in the classroom, the students absorb it thus affecting them adversely. Teaching is a tough task but when the teacher is passionate then teaching becomes easier. Teachers die but their teachings and messages never die as they pass from one generation to another. Hence, teachers are temporary but their teachings are eternal. That is the greatness of teaching. It is rightly said, "Teaching is the profession that teaches all the other professions."

Challenges for Youth

India will have 50 per cent of the population within the age of 25 years in the near future, and it is a healthy sign keeping the productivity and the progress of our country. When we look at the population of China it is ageing. In this context, India has a competitive edge over China. With the excellent base of young and productive population, India will progress rapidly despite having several challenges in other areas.

There are certain areas where youth need to improve such as the ability to dream big, think big, and act big. We have challenges like unemployability where we have ample of opportunities in employment, but we do not have employable youth to meet the skill sets of the employers. Employees are served with pink slips due to dearth of soft skills. Secondly, lack of encouragement in entrepreneurship is another challenge among Indian youth. Thirdly, students are not equipped with leadership qualities as we mostly have managers rather than leaders.

There is a need to focus on the present educational system which needs to be remodeled and reinvented as per the changing global scenario. Education which involves more of interaction, activities, and role-plays, with a practical approach can bring out the best in the students who can make country proud.

There is no doubt that the youth of this country is playing a crucial role in the growth of our nation. In fact, the future of any country lies in the hands of its youth. It is the teachers who must play a crucial role in shaping the students by becoming their role models and inspiring them to excel as great personalities. Hence, teachers must play diversified roles, and share their knowledge with students to shape them as successful citizens.

We will discuss the challenges for educators and students, various aspects of academic leadership, management education, success, coaching, and leadership in the following chapters.

REFERENCES

Author's Blogs:

http://professormsraoguru.blogspot.com

http://professormsrao.blogspot.com

http://profmsr.blogspot.com

2

Great Teachers are Born in the Hearts of the Students

> The mediocre teacher tells. The good teacher explains. The superior teacher demonstrates. The great teacher inspires.—*William Arthur Ward*

All teachers can't make impact in the minds of their students. But a very few teachers touch the hearts of their students and excel as great teachers. There is no specific formula or a secret mantra for their success except dedication, determination, and discipline in the methods of their teaching. Good teachers work with passion, and are totally involved in their profession and contribute their best without expecting any rewards or returns from their students except with a burning desire to be great at their profession. Many people think that teaching is an inborn quality to become a great teacher. It is a myth as people become great teachers through their passion, concentration, continuous learning, constant feedback, and above all, their sincere efforts to make a difference in the lives of students. A teacher is like a player of a musical instrument. S/he can produce either a sad music or a joyful music by playing the instrument. A good subject can be taught in a dull manner and a poor subject can be taught in an interesting way. Everything depends totally on the presentation of the player—teacher.

Type of Teachers

Teachers can be classified in various types such as good teacher versus bad teacher, friendly teacher versus hostile teacher, jovial teacher versus strict teacher, dominant teacher versus submissive teacher, serious teacher versus casual teacher to name a few.

According to R. Verdi, "Good teachers are those who know how little they know, bad teachers are those who think they know more than they don't know". The good teachers never boost nor boast of themselves. However, knowledgeable they might be, they think that what they know is only a drop of an ocean. Precisely, good teachers have humility. On the other hand, the bad teachers are poor performers who are not knowledgeable, and to hide their weaknesses, they pretend to be strong in their domain. This kind of teachers often blame their students for not concentrating in the class. It is like a bad tradesman who always blames his tools and never admits his incompetence.

A friendly teacher is always amenable, adjustable, and empathizes with their students and narrows down the gap between the teachers and the students to promote relations. Such a teacher is always accessible to the students for clarifying their doubts. In contrast, a hostile teacher is inimical, and his actions towards their students are reactive rather than proactive. They display unfriendly attitude when they hear from their students that other teachers are teaching better than him. Hostile teachers don't take criticism constructively.

The jovial teachers are filled with fun and humor. They entertain students with humor and anecdotes, and believe in imparting education in an entertaining manner. They do not get provoked, and take comments from their students jovially. While teaching, this kind of teacher believes in the carrot, not stick policy. This kind of teacher behaves from 'Child Ego State'. (According Dr. Berne, there are three types of ego states—'Patent Ego State', 'Adult Ego State' and Child Ego State', i.e. PAC Ego States.) On the other hand, the strict teachers are, no doubt, good teachers but they believe in stick rather than carrot policy in teaching. They expect the class to be in total silence, and they do not encourage their students to discuss on the topic among themselves. This kind of teachers are highly knowledgeable but uncompromising. They predominantly behave from their Parent Ego State.

The dominant teachers are again strict teachers but the degree of strictness is higher, and hence can also be called dictatorial or autocratic teachers. They are hardly concerned about the sentiments, views and opinions of their students. On the contrary, the submissive teachers are those who often succumb to the demands of their students, and they do not know how to control their students. Both these types are unwarranted and uncalled, and what is expected is the average of these two traits which can be called assertive teachers who strike a balance between dominant teachers and submissive teachers. An assertive teacher behaves from all the three ego states, i.e. the Parent, the Adult, and the Child Ego States as per the situation. It is rightly said, "The best teachers teach from heart, not from the book." An assertive teacher is an ideal teacher who teaches from her heart, and earns respect from students.

The serious teachers are, by nature, serious in their approach and they teach without adding any touch of humor but are very efficient and effective, and believe in professionalism. The students learn the topics in a professional manner. For this kind of teachers, work is worship. They mean business. On the contrary, the casual teachers take everything lightly, and may not be equipped with adequate knowledge, and believe in completing the syllabus and passing their time. This kind of teachers works for the sake of working and they never win the hearts of their students.

Characteristics of a Good Teacher

- Lola May quoted, "There are three things to remember when teaching; know your stuff, know whom you are stuffing; and then stuff them elegantly." Anybody can become a good teacher if stuffed with these things.

- A teacher wears many a hat as an effective communicator, leader, disciplinarian, mentor, guide, parent, friend, philosopher, motivator, counselor, actor, role model, well-wisher, and manager to name a few.
- Should not take students for granted.
- Should concentrate on all students equally.
- Should carry the entire students along with him as a team leader.
- A teacher should be thorough and well versed with the subjective knowledge and should share extra knowledge apart from his/her routine domain knowledge.
- Should have higher levels of energy and enthusiasm.
- Should remember the names of all students in the class.
- Should always work with sincerity and integrity.
- Should know how to present the topic based on common sense. If they find that some students don't fall in line they must call students privately for correction. On the other hand, if students contribute well they must be praised publicly. It serves as a positive stroke and the rest of the students will fall in line.
- A great teacher teaches, inspires, motivates and changes the mindsets of their students, and also the entire world. A great teacher always works with heart and head, as both are essential for effective teaching. A great teacher never demands but commands respect from his/her students.
- A great teacher is not only a teacher but also a great listener and learner. S/he teaches what s/he knows to his/her students and learns from what the students' know. Egotism is not the quality of a great teacher. A good teacher concentrates more on weak students rather than on bright students as Mara Collins said,

"The good teacher makes the poor student good and good student superior."

- A great teacher always sees the big picture. Whenever s/he finds that the topic is tough s/he breaks down the topic into several small pieces; explains the small pieces effectively to the students; and gradually assembles the pieces into a one single entity mentally and then explains. S/he should be a voracious reader of various books, magazines, journals, and browser of many educational websites.
- A great teacher is like a gardener who plants seeds, waters, and feels satisfied when plants become trees. S/he must be highly creative, dreamer, and must rise expectations and aspirations of his students. S/he emphasizes not only on education but also on ethical values and character building. S/he builds both subject and character among students.

Tools and Techniques of Teaching

> More important than the curriculum is the question of the methods of teaching and the spirit in which the teaching is given.—*Bertrand Russell*

A good teacher is always a good storyteller. S/he should start topic with a story and should gradually enter into the topic without the knowledge of the students and at the end of the session, only students should know that the teacher shared the relevant topics.

Students should feel that they entered into a theatre where they forget their real world problems the moment they enter the classroom. It all depends on the skills and abilities of the teacher.

A teacher may start the class with an interesting anecdote, or day-to-day happening report or a newspaper report or something shocking, and emotional everyday to draw the attention of their students.

A teacher can also start delivering lecture by role-playing, or referring an interesting case study or sharing his/her personal experience and with his/her industrial insights to bring students to the real life from the reel life.

S/he can also throw the topic for open discussion to get their views or opinions or comments about the topic. With this, the teacher is able to unearth the hidden talents lying in the subconscious minds of their students. It is like brainstorming the students to think innovatively, and imaginatively to ignite their minds. It is apt to quote Chinese proverb in this context, "Tell me and I'll forget, show me and I may remember, involve me and I will understand."

A good teacher always explains the concepts and fundamentals in depth as it serves as a strong infrastructure (foundation) over which students can build their superstructure.

Body language of the teacher must complement with his oral language as any inconsistency between them may create doubts in the minds of the students. Body language contributes 55 per cent, voice modulation contributes 38 per cent and oral language contributes 7 per cent of the communication. The combination of both body language with oral language helps communicate effectively with students. Although people talk many things orally, their body language often displays sincerity and integrity. The teacher must make use of his/her body language up to the hilt and, if required, s/he has to act in order to reach his/her students. Gail Godwin rightly said, "Good teaching is one-fourth preparation and three-fourth pure theatre."

A good teacher is a great democrat, and s/he often encourages students to participate in discussions and dialogue on the subject. S/he should be highly confident and comfortable while teaching.

A good teacher is an effective and efficient communicator and converts complex things into simple ones with his teaching tools. S/he tickles the students and enhances their creativity and innovation. If any student raises doubts, then the teacher asks other students in the classroom to clarify the query. If it is not clarified s/he must take responsibility and clarify through simple methods. In this method of teaching, the teacher provides an opportunity to other students to share their knowledge on the topics with students.

A good teacher blows away, if any myths in the minds of their students and should encourage and challenge them to touch their upper limits. A good teacher must be like a doctor with a healthy and positive mindset. Because when a patient goes to a doctor for taking medicine through syringe, the patient will have fear due to the pain syringe causes to the body. Then the doctor says nothing will happen by engaging the patient in a friendly chat, and injects the medicine into the body through the syringe. Similarly, if any topic is tough, the teacher must infuse confidence in his/her students by saying it as simple, and then should explain the concepts clearly with clarity of thought.

Teaching is nothing but a novel method of presenting the subject. One should know clearly that all successful teachers may not be knowledgeable teachers and all knowledge teachers may not be successful teachers.

A good teacher should be a great learner and s/he should be fully prepared on the topic by referring various books and then only s/he should enter the class as Joseph Joubert rightly said, "To teach is to learn twice."

A good teacher should not only know 'How to teach?' but should also know 'How to learn?' John Carolus S.J. rightly remarked, "We think too much about effective methods of teaching and not enough about effective methods of learning."

If necessary, a good teacher must carry audio, visual material, newspaper cuttings, to the class to experiment and experience the topic lively. The teacher should not be static on the dais like a statue; s/he must move his body from place to place to make the teaching natural and pleasant. In the middle of the teaching, s/he should ask appropriate questions about the topic to keep students agile, active, and alert in the class. Teacher must smile to put the students at ease.

S/he must link the topic from previous class to the present and to the future classes and there should be effective interconnectivity of the topic so that the students can feel that the subject is being taught with a natural flow. S/he should also ask questions from the previously discussed sessions so that the students will prepare seriously at home to avoid ambiguity and confusion in the class. If necessary, tests must be conducted periodically to ensure that the students study seriously at home and also to overcome any apprehensions during examinations.

When I took up teaching profession teaching on Management Science (MS) subject in an engineering college initially, I introduced myself formally with the students in the very first session. A student got up and asked me, "Sir, I did not hear your name properly and would you mind repeating your name?" Then I questioned the student to tell the name of the subject I was teaching. Student quickly replied it as, 'Management Science'. Then I asked the student to tell the name of the subject in abbreviated format. The student replied it as, 'MS'. Then I further asked the student to add Rao as suffix to M.S. I asked the student to tell my designation, and he quickly replied as, 'Professor' and then I asked him to prefix designation with M.S. Rao. By then the student had come to know my name as, 'Professor M.S. Rao'. This is also a way of teaching by questioning and involving students through a dialogue and discussion.

While teaching apart from the academic curriculum the students should be taught the practical application of the concepts. It is advisable to reconfirm from the students during the course of teaching by using close-ended questions such as 'Is that OK?', 'Is it clear?', 'Do you understand?', 'Is it alright?' and so on. It is a great technique to engage students in the classroom.

Conducting regular quiz programs or subject related quiz activities encourage the students to involve actively and briskly even at home about the academic studies. It is advisable to gift the bright students based on score they get during such programs. Or else, providing 'appreciation letters' or 'participation certificates' for such activities motivates them.

Teachers should respect their students and should hold them to high standards. Teachers should not snub students if they ask for any clarifications during the session. It is essential to conduct question-and-answer session at the end of each session by allocating some time. It is like taking stock of the session, and it often serves as a formal feedback. A teacher can also assess and gauge himself/herself how effectively s/he taught. A teacher should always stay focused on the subject. If warranted, it is necessary to repeat the key content to students.

A good teacher must step into the shoes of the students and must empathize. Offer model answers as guide, and it helps them to do well in the academic examinations. Preparation of various model answers is a must to have a feel of the examination. Teachers should adopt multiple teaching methodologies and strategies.

Why should Anyone Become a Teacher?

> Prior to being allowed to enter the profession, prospective teachers should be asked to talk with a group of friendly students for at least half an hour and be able to engage them in an interesting conversation about any subject the prospective teacher wants to talk about.—*William Glasser*

It is a noble profession and there is a great degree of sanctity attached to it. Most of the people take up this profession by chance, not by choice. When qualified candidates pass out from their institutions (who are also known as freshers) they search for employment. If they don't get any employment, they take teaching profession as a stopgap career. If the candidates like this profession they continue forever, or else, they make a career switch to other professions.

In fact, there is a sense of thrill while teaching to the students because shaping of students' future is only in the hands of the teachers. And a teacher can derive great sense of job satisfaction and achievement when s/he learns that his/her students achieved miracles in their career. Great teachers take pride in molding the future of their students.

This profession brings out both creativity and innovation to the fore both from the teachers and the students. Consciously or unconsciously, many hidden things unfold during the process of teaching. And one can tap one's own natural and creative potential spontaneously.

A teacher can feel like a commander till the completion of the class as the total students obey the teacher with discipline and dedication. Nobody can enter the classroom without his/her permission as s/he will have full command and control over it.

A teacher can also feel like a priest/pastor as the schools are treated as temples of learning thus attracting sanctity.

A teacher can learn his/her best from his/her students by posing various questions to the students thus generating multiple shades of views, opinions, ideas and comments on each topic. This will help grow richer in knowledge and stature.

A teacher can experiment various things in the classroom and can treat each teaching session as a workshop. S/he can adopt trial and error method for each experiment, and if s/he passes in the trial s/he can adopt the same strategies/tools in the next teaching sessions. If s/he fails, s/he can discard it. In a nutshell, a teacher can compare his/her classroom like laboratory for conducting various experiments.

In this profession, a teacher can wear many masks, like that of Hollywood stars who play different roles in their film career.

In this profession, one can enjoy maximum number of holidays, and can maintain work-life balance successfully. One can pursue writing books during holidays and leisure or can go for part time employment during long vacation. If possible, one can involve in experimentation of what s/he learned and taught in the classrooms in the outside world to create his/her own case studies.

Even if a teacher does not have sense of humor, the same can be cultivated by moving friendly with their students. One can feel young both in mind and heart as they move with students freely and frankly. By being with young people a teacher thinks very young all the time and s/he can work with higher levels of energy and enthusiasm.

Every profession is getting highly complex and complicated due to the growing technologies leading to higher levels of stress and burnout. In this profession, there is a least possibility of getting burnt out. Even if one gets stressed out, s/he can regain and recoup easily due to the availability of more leisure time.

As long as the teacher commands subject, s/he will command respect from their students, and superiors and it helps and ensures job security. So why not to choose this noble profession as a career option?

Great Teachers

A teacher should have passion, apply knowledge, and role-play with persuasive skills, presentation skills, and involvement, to excel as a great teacher.

An average teacher teaches the topic, a good teacher converts dull students into bright students, and a great teacher creates great students who in turn excel in their chosen areas. And such great teachers become teaching legends. Alexander the Great quoted, "I am indebted to my father for living, but to my teacher for living well." The great teachers across the globe are Aristotle, Galileo, Isaac Newton, and Pythogorous to name a few. They are great because they contributed their best in their lifetimes.

How to Become a Successful Teacher?

> When you study great teachers...you will learn much more from their caring and hard work than from their style.—*William Glasser*

Think of teachers those who made an impact in your mind right from your childhood. Find out the reasons what made them so memorable in your minds. Recollect the tools, techniques, strategies, methodologies which made prints in your mind. Analyze one by one slowly, and list out: Gradually apply them in your practical life whenever you get an opportunity. Ignite passion in the minds of the students. Inculcate and cultivate out-of-the-box thinking, by traveling the uncharted path to leave a mark behind. Always think, dream and sleep over the novel methods of teaching. With interest and through regular interactions with students, one can evolve one's own methods of teaching. Read and reread the books of great teachers across the world to find out what made them stand out from others. Also browse websites on teaching to gain more knowledge.

Look at your strengths and weaknesses and overcome your weaknesses by regular practice and training. Take active part in various seminars, workshops and training programs to learn continuously. Especially in such wonderful workshops, the birds of the same feather flock together. And that is again a wonderful platform to interact and learn many things.

Regularly take feedback from your students, and find out the key areas that needs improvement. Students are the source of strength for any teacher. The students' mindsets are not controlled and conditioned. They are young, fresh and energetic with virgin minds. They are far away from preconceived notions and views. Their views and comments are authentic and genuine.

The feedback covers many areas such as body language, communication skills, relevance, examples, data, and novelty. Also take feedback from your subordinates, peers, and superiors and discuss with them regularly the ways and means to bring out the best in you and also in your students.

According to the Hindu philosophy, the mother comes first (*Matrudevo Bhava*), the father comes second (*Pitrudevo Bhava*), and the teacher comes third (*Acharyadevo Bhava*) in status. The teacher is accorded one of the highest statuses, and it is indeed a great honor to teachers. To summarize, teachers are not born, but with practice, they can be made. The great teachers are not born in the minds of their students but they are born in the hearts of their students.

REFERENCES

Author's Blogs:

http://professormsraoguru.blogspot.com

http://professormsrao.blogspot.com

http://profmsr.blogspot.com

3

How to Teach Well, and Motivate Students?

> The average teacher explains complexity; the gifted teacher reveals simplicity.—*Robert Brault*

Teaching is an art, and it requires tons of passion to teach students. Having mere knowledge to impart is not enough. In order to become a competent and successful teacher, it is essential to understand the roles and responsibilities of teachers, the skills and styles of teaching, tools and techniques of teaching, right usage of evaluation techniques, the psychology of the students, and the ability to motivate the students. When a teacher knows them properly he or she can become not only a good teacher but also a great leader by transferring knowledge, experience, skills and abilities from one generation to another generation through students.

Role of a Teacher

Every teacher dons many a hat. S/he teaches the subject or topic and imparts knowledge to the students. That is the primary role and responsibility of the teacher. S/he also acts as a friend, philosopher, guide, parent, and facilitator. S/he is a continuous learner and constant listener. The more s/he listens, the more s/he learns, and the more s/he learns, the more s/he teaches. That is why it is said that the teachers must be lifelong learners.

Teaching Styles

Teaching styles[1] can be categorized as: formal authority, demonstrator or personal model, facilitator, and delegator.

In the formal authority, the prepared content is delivered by the teacher to the students according to the syllabus. In this style, the interaction is the least and the delivery of the content is the most. No connections are made between the teachers and the students. It is delivered formally by the teacher.

In the second style of demonstrator, the teacher demonstrates to the students empirically to enable students to understand and learn easily. For solving any mathematical problem, the teacher uses the formula, solves the problem, and asks the students to solve other problems. Similarly, the technical students can learn in the laboratory the methodology through demonstration by the teacher so that the students can learn and apply the same.

In the third style of facilitator, the teacher encourages the students to involve in activities like role-plays, discussion, and participation in classroom to facilitate learning environment. Here the students learn themselves and the teacher only facilitates the learning environment. This is often meant for independent learners. The trainers usually apply this style to enable the skills and abilities to the trainees.

In the fourth style of delegator, teacher gives tasks to the students and asks them to execute their tasks either individually or collectively by forming groups. The students are provided with various options to choose and learn. The students learn by themselves as the teacher gives them freedom to learn by delegating.

We cannot rush to conclusion that a particular teaching style is proper and appropriate. It all depends on the nature of the teacher, the profile of the students, the discipline, and the situation that makes sense of usage of a specific style of teaching.

Teaching Skills

Teaching is a skill, not a talent. Anybody and everybody can cultivate this skill. Before teaching in the classroom, it is necessary to profile the students, and find out what are their requirements, expectations and aspirations. Once this is done effectively then create the content accordingly.

The first and foremost thing is to have a clarity of the concept. Once it is formed and framed properly, look at its suitability and relevance for the students. Then make sure that the content is relevant and appropriate to the students.

Structuring and sequencing the content should be proper in a chronological order with key concepts, examples, and anecdotes. It comes under organizing the course content in a methodical manner.

As discussed in the previous chapter, Socratic Method as a tool of teaching is very interesting for the students. When students pose questions, the teacher should teach them by providing answers usually generated from their questions by way of interaction, introspection, and deep grilling. It helps the students unlock their hidden potential and engage them actively into the teaching process. Succinctly, the teaching skills vary from person to person depending on his or her style, nature and also on the domain, topic, and on the profile of the students. There is no fixed or regimented teaching formula in teaching skills.

Teaching Methodology

> It must be remembered that the purpose of education is not to fill the minds of students with facts...it is to teach them to think, if that is possible, and always to think for themselves.—*Robert Hutchins*

During teaching, the teacher should adopt various tools and techniques to ensure effective teaching outcomes. The teacher can start the topic with an interesting or shocking statement or an inspiring event or happening. It is also desirable if the teacher starts with a short story to arouse interest among the students. If the teacher takes the session for the first time, it is advisable to break the ice by asking about the profile of the students. If the classes are conducted routinely, it is desirable to question the students by asking them about what was discussed in the previous sessions to link the previous session with the present session. It helps in breaking the ice and connecting the students naturally to the present thus ensuring smooth connectivity.

Once the ice has been broken gradually, the teacher should deliver the content by maintaining equal eye contact with all students. It helps the teacher gauge the body language of the students. If any unfavorable signals are noticed the teacher must explain the same once again, and gauge their body language for smooth takeaways. If it is favorable, the teacher can proceed further. If the body language of the students is still not favorable then the teacher has to revise his/her style of teaching style to suit with students' expectations. Once it is okay then the teacher should pose questions intermittently to draw the attention of the students. Giving adequate pauses during teaching helps students understand better as they can paraphrase the delivered contents.

The teacher should keep reserve content ready to ensure smooth flow of teaching if the regular content is dried up. If the reserve content is not ready then the teacher should involve students through questioning and interaction. The teacher should encourage the students to shoot questions about the topic. It helps students to be active in their learning process and to think deeper and better.

During the teaching process, the teacher should be cool and composed, and should ensure that the students are aroused with enthusiasm and interest. The teacher must make sure that the students are inspired from teaching.

Motivating Students

> A teacher who is attempting to teach without inspiring the pupil with a desire to learn is hammering on cold iron.—*Horace Mann*

Motivating students is not a child's play, and it is indeed a Herculean task. The teacher must motivate and inspire the students by being a role model and through various innovative and creative teaching methods. Here are the ways how a teacher can motivate and inspire the students:

First of all, it is necessary to know the names of the students as it creates connection with the students. Everyone loves to be recognized by his/her name. The sweetest thing in the world is one's own name. This is just the beginning of building bridges and developing rapport with the students.

Find out what motivates the students and what are their aspirations and expectations from the teacher. Every teacher is knowledgeable, and is strong in his/her domain. But it alone does not work out. What works out is the ability to find the needs of the students and deliver the same. In this process, it is necessary to gauge the pulse of the students. The needs of every student are different. The knack involved is to find out the same, and cater the same effectively and efficiently.

The teacher should have good energy levels and demonstrate the same during teaching. This helps the students take interest in the topic and encourages them involving in the teaching process.

During the delivery of the content, the flow has to be lively, smooth, and natural filled with real life examples and the rags-to-riches stories. This inspires them think in a big way; enhances their imagination levels; and touch their tipping points. The thought process must be chronological connecting with various ideas with smooth transitions. It helps them understand the content better thus eliminating any room for doubts.

Set goals in such a way that the goals are realistic and achievable. It helps them attempt the goals and move further thus building their confidence levels. Once they reach their goals, appreciate them, and set bigger goals where they find it challenging.

Giving feedback continuously helps students improve themselves. It is necessary to offer praise immediately and instantly when they achieve something and that too in public as it boosts their self-esteem. If the feedback to be given is negative, it is proper to call privately and provide it. While giving negative feedback, it is essential to depersonalize it. The intention is to attack the issue, not the individual. The intention is to attack the behavior of the individuals, not the individuals. Even in this, it is proper to provide sandwich feedback. That is start with a compliment, embed correcting the negative behavior, and close with a compliment.

Writing on the blackboard daily with a motivational quote will help the students break the ice and get motivated. When such quotes are given daily to the students, it sends right signals, and fills their mind with intellectual and inspirational inputs, and above all, it helps in everlasting impact in the minds of the students.

Start the session with a motivational story as it conveys morals and inspires them. We humans love to listen stories, and storytelling is an art every teacher has to master to cater to the students. Along with the story share the knowledge about the subject or topic. Often storytelling breaks the ice and initiates the teaching process.

Conduct quizzes, debates, and brainstorming sessions by keeping the profile of the students in view. It creates informal learning environment and promotes healthy competition among the students. It brings you closer to the students. It gives extra knowledge and information apart from the knowledge about the curriculum. Giving small prizes to the winners and some consolation prizes to others will encourage other students to participant in such activities. Such initiatives will help in bonding with the students forever.

The teacher has equally a challenging role in motivating the dull or shy or introvert students. The teacher should regularly put in the extra efforts to focus on such students. The teacher should encourage this segment of students to initiate a dialogue to get the desired outcomes. In this world, there are few people who allow others to talk and the majority of the people talk about themselves. When the teacher encourages such students to talk then they would be happy to open up their minds and gradually get streamlined along with other bright and active students.

Empathize with the students by stepping into their shoes. Understand what their needs, wants, drives and motives. Listen to them carefully and motivate them.

Be warm and friendly with students. Call them personally to your personal cabin and talk to them closely what they want and what extra they would like to learn. Despite time constraints, give them your best to earn their respect.

It is improper to compare one student with another student as it creates differences among the students. It leads to ego clashes among the students. Everyone is unique in this world. Even twins are not alike. Then how can we expect all students to be alike or how can we compare one student with another?

The teacher must sympathize with the students who fail in the examinations. S/he should encourage such students by helping them in realizing their hidden potential. There is a need to diagnose the reasons of failure, and help the students overcome the drawbacks in their learning methods.

Teaching Evaluation

Teacher can evaluate either by observing the body language of the students or asking informally the students outside the class. Instead of questioning about the effectiveness of his or her teaching style or method, the teacher must ask the students whether there are any suggestions for improvement or if there are further areas to be covered. It helps in finding out the gaps existing in their teaching process or methodology. If such questions are asked in the classroom, students may not respond in the presence of all. For effective evaluation, it is better to associate with the students informally, and take their feedback. Even if the students come out with negative feedback it should not be taken personally but should be taken professionally for improvement. Hence, it is advisable to take feedback from students through informal discussions.

Teaching is a noble profession. It is the teacher who connects the knowledge from one generation to another generation through students. If the teacher possesses the depth of the knowledge in one domain, the students' possess the breadth of the knowledge in various domains and that makes the difference between the teacher and the students. The teacher shapes and moulds the characters of the students by teaching. One cannot expect huge money in this profession but one can expect great respect and regards. The amount of satisfaction is indeed immense when taught with passion. When teacher goes extra mile with extra efforts by motivating and inspiring the students, s/he will earn great respect from students.

NOTE

1. http://membes.shaw.ca/mdde615/tchstyles/htm. as accessed on 11 November 2008.

REFERENCES

http://professormsraoguru.blogspot.com

http://professormsrao.blogspot.com

http://profmsr.blogspot.com

http://members.shaw.ca/mdde615/tchstyles.htm

http://www.ntlf.com/html/lib/faq/ts-indiana.htm

4

Meka's Method®—An Innovative Teaching Tool

> First, have a definite, clear practical ideal; a goal, an objective. Second, have the necessary means to achieve your ends; wisdom, money, materials, and methods. Third, adjust all your means to that end.—*Aristotle*

Since time immemorial, various teachers and educators created several teaching tools, techniques, and methodologies to ensure successful takeaways for students. For instance, there is an education instruction named Socratic Method. It is a form of inquiry and debate to stimulate critical thinking and ignite ideas. Based on Socratic Method, oil magnet and philanthropist, Edward Harkness developed a teaching style—Harkness Method in early 1930s. It is far away from conventional classroom teaching of chalkboard lecturing to students. It helps teachers immensely as they don't continuously teach due to the active involvement of students in the teaching process. This method develops critical thinking among the students and promotes public speaking skills apart from building their confidence levels. It is a win-win for both teachers and students as students acquire knowledge from other students and build confidence among themselves, and teachers acquire new ideas and insights from students.

In Harkness Method, no single student dominates the session as everyone gets an opportunity to have a dialogue on the topic. It calls for an oval table around which approximately thirteen students and an instructor sit. The teacher shoots thought-provoking questions or topics that the group discusses. This method encourages shy students to come forward and voice their views and opinions. It is followed in many American schools. It is also known as modern application of Socratic Method.

Here is another innovative teaching tool I have coined—'Meka's Method' in 2007. It is a structured and methodical way of teaching where the content is delivered on a platter as per the context and situation to ensure effective teaching outcomes. It is a democratic method of teaching where the teaching is by the students, for the students, and of the students as this teaching method involves students' participation, cooperation, interaction, communication, collaboration, summarization, and contribution. The teacher serves as a facilitator and moderator and ensures that the students are actively involved in the teaching process, and are assured of teaching outcomes. It is also a situational teaching as the teacher moulds his/her teaching style as per the learning styles and profiles of students and changes the style from time to time within the classroom by gauging at the mood and grasping level of the students. It blends education, entertainment, and all ingredients proportionately to ensure effective teaching takeaways among the students. Before we discuss in depth about Meka's Method we will understand the importance of new teaching tools and methods.

Importance of New Teaching Tools

> More important than the curriculum is the question of the methods of teaching and the spirit in which the teaching is given.—*Bertrand Russell*

Novel teaching techniques encourage students to take part actively in the learning process, and help in uncorking their hidden potential as they think intelligently, and apply the theory into practice effectively. Studies have made it clear that the students' achievement, excellence, and success depends on having experienced and trained teachers who have a passion to make a difference in their lives. Therefore, teachers must do research, update and innovate themselves constantly to create new teaching tools and techniques to succeed academically, otherwise they will be made obsolete. They must understand various learning styles of students and mould their teaching style as per the students' needs to create a compatibility and chemistry between the teachers and the students.

What is 'Meka's Method'?

> I have come to believe that a great teacher is a great artist and that there are as few as there are any other great artists. Teaching might even be the greatest of the arts since the medium is the human mind and spirit. —*John Steinbeck*

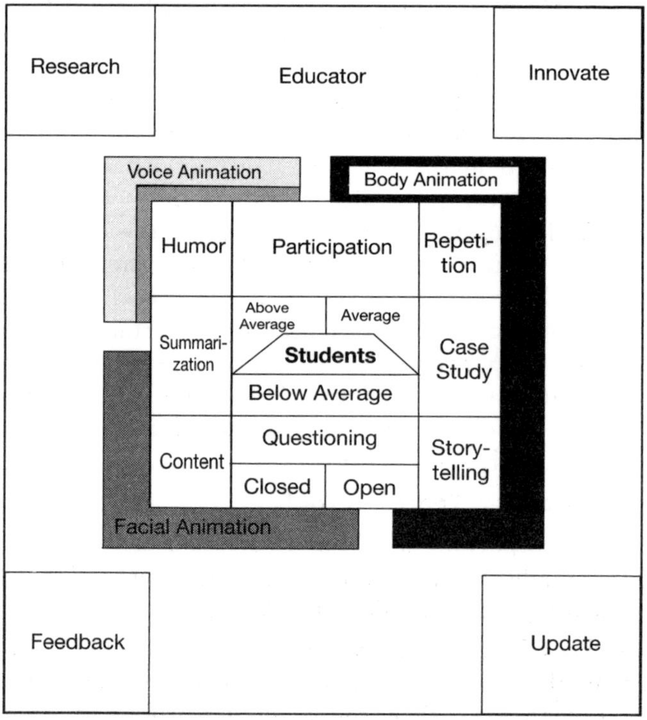

Figure 1: Meka's Method®

In this method of teaching as outlined in Figure 1, the teachers use their body animation, voice animation, facial animation along with interaction, questioning, and involving students' participation, taking feedback from their body language, and molding the teaching strategy as per the situation to ensure effective teaching outcomes.

Studies unfold that people remember 20 per cent of what they hear, 30 per cent of what they see, 50 per cent of what they hear and see, and 80 per cent of what they hear, see and do. It is obvious from this study that it is essential to blend audio, video, and interaction to ensure effective teaching outcomes. Hence, while teaching, usage of blackboard is essential as it provides effective visual effects and the human brain remembers more when presented with visual effects rather than with auditory effects. In fact, some students are auditory learners and some are visual learners. Studies unfold that most of the students are visual learners rather than auditory learners. Hence, even if the students fail to understand the oral language, the writing material on the blackboard will help them understand and retain the information effectively. While using the blackboard, the teacher should not spend too much time looking at the blackboard as the teacher loses connectivity with the students. There must be proper coordination between the blackboard writing and oral language of the teacher to accomplish teaching goals and objectives successfully.

The adage, "A picture is worth a thousand words" is apt in 'Meka's Method' because students remember better with visual pictures rather than in vocal sounds. The eyes are more powerful than ears. In addition, it helps in visualization and connecting the reel content with the real life events and experience quickly. Therefore, teachers must make use of showing visual pictures while teaching.

In listening, there is a popular term, 'Time Lag'. It is the gap between what a sender can speak and a receiver can listen. Human brain is a powerful and wonderful device, and it accepts 500-600 words per minute on an average whereas the speaker can deliver between 125 to 150 words per minute on an average. Epictetus rightly quoted, "We have two ears and one mouth so that we can listen twice as much as we speak." This gap between the speaking and listening rate is known as 'Time Lag'. It is also known as 'Word Lag'.

Apart from visual and auditory effects, the teacher should question the students about the topic in the middle of the teaching. The teacher must pose both close-ended and open-ended questions to keep the students glued to the teaching process. In order to ensure successful flow while teaching, the teacher must use close-ended questions such as 'Do you understand me?', 'Am I clear to you?', 'Is that clear to you?', 'Does it make sense?', If the teacher finds that the students' body language is not positive the way s/he expected, the teacher may shoot open-ended questions to a few students by giving break to teaching process such as 'Could you explain what I said?', 'What did you understand about the topic?', 'How can you apply the discussed learning in your real life events?'. It keeps students alert as they become proactive with open-ended questions and listen more attentively as the teacher asks questions. It helps them to think through the topic, and develops their thinking skills. It widens their mental faculties, and helps them relate theory with practical life. It prevents students' mind from wandering due to 'Time Lag', and they summarize what the teacher has taught and keeps them totally immersed in the classroom. In this regard, it is apt to recall the quote of William Glasser: "This is at the heart of all good education, where the teacher asks students to think and engages them in encouraging dialogues, constantly checking for understanding and growth."

The teacher must touch upon the topic systematically and chronologically by arousing curiosity from the beginning to the end of the session. S/he must maintain high levels of energy and enthusiasm throughout the teaching session. S/he must ensure students' mental presence in the class by referring relevant case studies, conducting role-plays, narrating personal examples, sharing anecdotes or telling stories. Storytelling is an art, and if the teacher narrates inspiring stories which are message-oriented and theme-oriented, the students will take more interest and listen attentively. Apart from sharing knowledge, the storytelling quickly connects theory with practice, and brings excitement among the students.

While delivering the content, the teacher must repeat the key ideas thrice as in every classroom we find three kinds of students. The first kind of audience is of above average, the second kind is of average, and the third kind is of below average students. When teacher emphasizes the key ideas and concepts three times, s/he must be able to touch three kinds of students equally thus doing total justification to teaching.

At the end of sharing knowledge, the teacher must call a few volunteers in the classroom to summarize what was taught in the classroom. It helps reinforce the takeaways. In addition, the poor listeners and students with low intelligence levels will benefit from such summarization. The teacher must also encourage the students who are introvert by nature or non-participant due to shyness to summarize key essence of the content. It helps such students break their silence and come forward with more confidence. Mark Van Doren rightly remarked, "The art of teaching is the art of assisting discovery."

The teacher should be flexible in his or her body movements and move around freely with a friendly smile to encourage students' participation. The flexible body movements of teacher will make the teaching session lively and interesting to the students. The teacher must possess humor quotient and include humor in the teaching process. There are innumerable advantages with humor as it breaks the ice with students, relieves them from the listening stress, refreshes their minds, and connects quickly with the content. The teacher must interconnect and apply diversified tools and techniques as per the situation to make the teaching process a pleasant and memorable one. This entire process of teaching where the teacher uses audio, visual, storytelling, humor, interaction, and questioning by engaging students, repetition of key ideas, and summarization of the entire content in the classroom to ensure effective teaching goals and objectives is known as *Meka's Method* of teaching.

It is a fact that one-size-fits-all type of education doesn't work, and the 21st century education calls for novel teaching methodologies where teachers must mould themselves as per the students' intelligence levels and situation. In fact, there is need for situational teaching. John Howells, rightly remarked, "Education is no longer about children sitting in rows in front of a blackboard with the teacher imparting wisdom and the children taking it all down like it was the Holy Writ. Times have changed—children have changed—and schools need to change with them."

Encourage Students to Think

Plutarch said, "The mind is not a vessel to be filled but a fire to be ignited." Hence, teachers should not dump knowledge in the minds of students. They must encourage their students to think. Only when students think they will be able to differentiate between knowledge and information, and appreciate true knowledge and acquire it. They also think various ways to apply the acquired knowledge in their real lives. In fact, application of knowledge is more important than acquisition of knowledge. Teachers must shoot questions in the classroom to widen students' mental faculties. They must probe students to the maximum possible extent so that students are awakened and interested in the classroom learning.

Conclusion

Clay P. Bedford quoted, "You can teach a student a lesson for a day; but if you can teach him to learn by creating curiosity, he will continue the learning process as long as he lives." The role of teachers has widened as previously teachers taught students the art of catching the fish to enable students to become competent and independent. However, the present-day teachers must not only teach the art of catching the fish to their students but also show the location of the fish so that students are benefitted immensely. Hence, teachers must discharge their roles and responsibilities keeping with the current aspirations and expectations of students in view.

Currently, students have higher expectations and aspirations due to the rapid growth in technology. They discard the old things, and want everything new. Previously, the teaching strategy was based on 'chalk and talk' which doesn't work in the current context. Hence, we need to create new tools and techniques as per the changing tastes, aspirations, and expectations of students. Remember that the old teaching tools that worked in the past may not work currently. Hence, there is a need for creating new teaching tools and methods to carry forward education from one generation to another generation successfully with value addition. Alan McMurdo rightly said, "Kids have higher expectations these days and they can multi-task and access new technology to a degree—and at a speed—that adults can only dream of, so if education is to remain relevant to them, we have to adapt, whether we like it or not." To conclude, teachers must remember that if they give more than the students wanted, they will get more than what they expected. Hence, teach from the core of your heart to impact, influence and inspire your students to stand out as an academic leader.

Acknowledgements

I thank my two sons—Meka Ganesh Sai and Meka Ramakrishna Sayee for their contribution to this innovative teaching tool—Meka's Method.

REFERENCES

Author's Blogs:

http://professormsraoguru.blogspot.com

http://professormsrao.blogspot.com

http://profmsr.blogspot.com

5

Classroom Management

> If there is any other situations fraught with danger for mental health as that of a class held rigid by fear, it is a class exposed to the anxieties engendered by unlimited freedom. There is nothing as terrifying to the immature human being as a completely unstructured situation. Without a recognizable structure they feel the teacher has abandoned them—and so he has—to their own impulses, all of which are by no means always constructive.—*B. Morris*

According to Skinner,[1] "We are on the verge of a new educational method a new pedagogy in which the teacher will emerge as a skilled behavioral engineer. He will be able to analyze the contingencies, which will arise in his classroom and design and set up improved versions. He will know what is to be done and will have the satisfaction of knowing that he has done it."

For every teacher, managing classroom is one of the biggest challenges. For most of the people it appears easy to maintain discipline in the classroom. But in reality it is a tough task for the teacher as s/he cannot afford to incur the ill-will of their students by enforcing discipline. At the same time it is essential to maintain discipline and decency in the classroom to impart the knowledge successfully. In this context, let us look at the meaning of classroom management.

What is Classroom Management?

According to Wikipedia, classroom management[2] is a term used by many teachers to describe the process of ensuring that classroom lessons run smoothly despite disruptive behavior by students. The term also implies the prevention of disruptive behavior. It is possibly the most difficult aspect of teaching for many teachers and indeed experiencing problems in this area causes some to leave teaching altogether. In 1981, the US National Educational Association reported that 36 per cent of teachers said they would probably not go into teaching if they had to decide again. A major reason was "negative student attitudes and discipline" (Wolfgang and Glickman).

From this report, it is obvious that classroom indiscipline has become a major concern for the teachers. It is surprising to note that just because of classroom issues teachers do not like to pursue teaching as a career.

In a nutshell, classroom management can be defined as the process of disciplining, interacting, educating, entertaining, eliciting and integrating the students in a constructive and creative class environment for providing knowledge, skills and abilities. The sole objective of classroom management is to provide favorable learning environment for the students. It basically revolves around three factors like discipline, motivation, and respect. Only when the students are disciplined, motivated and respected, we can ensure effective classroom environment.

Six Cs for a Teacher

Every teacher should have six Cs such as courage, competence, confidence, communication, commitment, and concern. The ability to face a huge number of students requires courage, and at the same time the teacher should have managing, controlling, and commanding skills. Teacher not only teaches but also plays several roles in the class. Courage is needed to play these multiple roles. Competence is one of the core areas, and it is one of the major characteristics of any teacher. Competence comes only when the teacher is thorough with the subject knowledge. And the competence in turn leads to confidence. Students may pose several questions, and the teacher should display confidence levels to respond the same. However, competent the teacher may be, s/he should be able to communicate the same to the students effectively to share his/her knowledge. What is the use of having extensive knowledge when the teacher doesn't know how to communicate? The teacher should have commitment towards his/her professional roles and responsibilities. It earns respect from students. And about the sixth C—concern, the teacher should have concern about the students whether they understand the topics taught in the class. It is possible to know by observing the body language of the students. Therefore, all six Cs are crucial for all teachers.

Teaching Methodologies

> The number one problem in the classrooms is not discipline; it is lack of authentic learning tasks, procedures and routines.—*Harry Wong*

Every teacher has unique way of teaching, as no two teachers are alike. However, there are certain teaching and training methodologies that can be adopted which are common in nature. After following the same one can evolve one's own teaching methodologies based on experience and expertise, and research.

Any teaching should have combination of audio, video, interaction, questioning, case studies or examples or short stories, and summary. All these ingredients are essential more or less in any classroom teaching, and the same may be customized based on the profile of the students and the domain one belongs. Every teacher speaks in the class, which can be called an audio, and at the same time the teacher should use blackboard or power point presentations or cue cards to support the audio version of teaching. Only when these two are effectively coordinated and synchronized along with case study or short story, with active interaction and questioning the teaching will be complete and effective. At the end, encouraging the students to summarize what was discussed will make the teaching process highly effective.

Innovative Teaching Tips

> I cannot teach anybody anything, I can only make them think.—*Socrates*

Here are the tips teacher must follow to teach effectively and earn respect from their students.

- Maintain a diary exclusively for collecting motivational and inspirational quotations and share one quote for one session to the students regularly. It helps in motivating and inspiring the students.
- Maintain a diary exclusively for collecting short stories and use it in the classroom to fill the gaps, if any, during the classroom teaching. We humans love to listen to stories and any small story which is message-oriented will arouse interest among the students, and helps in character building.
- Daily teach one new word or concept other than the domain, which indicates your interest in teaching and encourages the students to learn new terminologies or concepts on regular basis. It also helps in widening the knowledge base of the students.

Action Exercises

> In an effective classroom students should not only know what they are doing, they should also know why and how.—*Harry Wong*

Here is an exercise that triggers students into action. Ask a question like "What gives you 100 per cent success?" and then invite their answers, and probably students may come out with words like discipline, knowledge, experience, commitment, intelligence....

Then give the answer as "ATTITUDE" and justify by telling students as follows: Number the alphabets of English from 1 to 26 with A assigning with number 1, B assigning with number 2 and at the end Z assigning with number with 26. Then assign each number against each letter in the word "ATTITUDE" and then sum it up, and it comes to 100. Therefore, the answer is—ATTITUDE gives you 100 success.

Likewise design your own exercises that enthuse and excite the students and help in sharing knowledge and maintaining classroom discipline.

Tools and Techniques for Favorable Classroom Management

> First, understand that behavior and classroom management are two different things. Behavior has to do with discipline. Classroom management has to do with procedures and routines.—*Harry Wang*[3]

- If the teachers possess competency in their subject, the students will fall in line of discipline and respect their teachers.
- Teachers should command rather than demand respect from students.
- It is necessary to have proper rapport with students. It minimizes any gap in understanding between the teachers and students thus promoting classroom harmony and peace.
- According to Emmer[4] and colleagues, assertive behavior is the ability to stand up for one's legitimate rights in ways that make it less likely that others will ignore or circumvent them (2003, p. 146). Teachers need to be assertive right from the beginning as it conveys right attitude towards them thereby having longevity in understanding and maintaining relations. There should not be any aggressive or submissive behavior in the initial stage as it conveys wrong signals to the students.
- Teachers should memorize the names so that they can address their students by their names to bond with them.
- Teachers should set personal example in their behavior. If students find any gap between what the teachers preach and practice the teachers will lose their credibility. In the long run, it leads to classroom indiscipline.

- Knowing the students' psychology will help the teachers behave amicably and further better relations between the teachers and the students.
- Teachers should be good time managers and should not waste their time in unproductive and meaningless discussions. They should be punctual to their classrooms.
- Avoid classroom politics and treat all students equally irrespective of their merits, ranks and social positions.
- If students misbehave, the teachers should use their body language with serious facial expressions, and eye contact to express as a sign of displeasure.
- Teachers can give notes to students to control commotion in the classroom.
- Teachers can engage their students the moment they enter the classroom by writing one or two questions on the board. They can ask the questions to students so that the students start thinking to respond. It checks the classroom commotion.
- The teachers can also crack jokes and direct classroom from commotion to normalcy as students enjoy the jokes.
- The teachers can ask students about the topics that have been discussed in the previous session as it quickly engages the students, and controls the classroom commotion.
- In the larger interests of permanent classroom management, the teachers should list out their expectations from their students and at the same time they should find out the expectations of the students. If there are any gaps between the expectations and realities teachers must bridge the same. This democratic style of discussion and interaction between the teachers and the students will promote healthy relations. It helps in ensuring the teaching objectives effectively and efficiently.

- Teachers should be equipped with adequate material in order to engage the students effectively. There should be material on practical activities, role-plays, short stories, case studies, etc., which can be utilized as per the situation to fill the gaps in the class. It will help especially when the topic is totally covered and teacher gets dry with the topic material.
- In extreme cases, when the student does not fall in line with the established discipline despite repeated reminders for correction of behavior then the last resort would be to bring the issue to the parents for their immediate action and correction. This weapon would be used as a last resort when all the options failed to pay off. Such an action will send strong signal to other students in the class, and they would be set right automatically.

Giving Feedback

Giving feedback to the students is a very challenging and tough job for teachers. It must be given without hurting them personally. However, if it is praise it is necessary to praise in public, and if it is criticism then it is advisable to call personally to cabin and criticize privately. While giving feedback it is necessary to attack the behavior of the student, not the student to bring out behavioral improvement.

While praising it should be objective and specific. That means pinpoint the specific act that resulted in positive outcome, and then praise. Otherwise, it sounds like a flattery and the receiver does not take it seriously. Any pat has to be appropriate and timely. Hence, observe and applaud the good behavior to make your praise to be effective. And do it in the presence of other students so that other students demonstrate similar positive behavior. In this way, the teacher not only praises the behavior of a particular student but also encourages others indirectly to emulate best practices.

Sandwich feedback is another tool that can be employed effectively in correcting the students to ensure effective classroom management. In this feedback, initially the teachers offer the positive compliment, and highlight the negative behavior for correction, and finally conclude with positive compliment. In this way, the students do not get hurt, and take the feedback constructively for effective improvement. Here is an example of sandwich feedback:

"Dear Robert, you often score good marks in the examinations. However, in the recent examinination you did not score well. It is time for you to pull up your socks. And I am sure you will definitely improve your score in the next examination."

Handling Question-and-Answer Session

Honesty is the best policy. When a student poses questions about the subject, the teacher must be in a position to reply up to the satisfaction of the student. It is possible only when the teacher is strong in the subject. If the answer to the question is not known, it is better to say that the answer would be addressed in the next session. It is not possible to know everything under the sun on the earth. It is mandatory to prepare fully the answer from various dimensions to respond to the student. It not only enhances the credibility of the teacher but also helps enhance the knowledge base. Another way of responding the answer is to ask any other students in the classroom to reply the question, and pass on the credit to the student upon receiving the right answer. Even if the answer is known to the teacher, then also the same question may to be passed on to other students to respond, and if any student provides partially correct answer then the teacher can summarize the answer totally up to the satisfaction of the student. It helps in enhancing the interaction and maintaining classroom discipline.

A.P.J. Abdul Kalam reminds, "A student spends 25,000 hours in the campus. The school must have the best of teachers who have the ability to teach, love teaching and build moral qualities." It means considerable amount of time is spent in the campus only. Hence, teachers must make conducive learning environment for students. When best practices and procedures are adopted, it is easy to manage classroom effectively thereby making learning process easier. There has to be openness, right coordination, and synchronization among the teachers, students, parents, and administration to maintain classroom discipline. To conclude in the words of Sylvia Ashton Warner, "The word 'freedom' can never be uttered unless accompanied hand in hand with the word responsibility. It is kinder to keep the lid on the school for a start, lifting it little by little, simultaneously teaching responsibility, until the time comes when the lid can be cast entirely aside and only two conditions remain—freedom and responsibility."

NOTES

1. www.fiu.edu/~pelaeznm/images/Resource/Martha/EEX%204601%20Instructor's%20Notes/Unit_1_EDP3218.ppt as accessed on 02 Sep. 2008.
2. http://en.wikipedia.org/wiki/Classroom_management as accessed on 03 Sep. 2008.
3. https://www.acsi.org/webfiles/webitems/attachments/002072_Classroom%20Management.ppt as accessed on 02 Sep. 2008.
4. http://books.google.co.in/books?id=s5S3ixTQw3YC&pg=PA28&lpg=PA28&dq=%C2%B7% as accessed on 01 Sep. 2008.

REFERENCES

http://professormsraoguru.blogspot.com

http://professormsrao.blogspot.com

http://profmsr.blogspot.com

www.fiu.edu/~pelaeznm/images/Resource/Martha/EEX%204601%20Instructor's%20Notes/Unit_1_EDP3218.ppt

http://en.wikipedia.org/wiki/Classroom_management

http://www.usingenglish.com/forum/teaching-english/54168-good-teacher-like-candle-consumes-itself-light-way-others-3.html

https://www.acsi.org/webfiles/webitems/attachments/002072_Classroom%20Management.ppt

http://books.google.co.in/books?id=s5S3ixTQw3YC&pg=PA28&lpg=PA28&dq=%C2%B7%

www.chench.com/quotes/teachers-and-teaching-children

6

Cue Cards are Clue Cards

> He is one of those orators of whom it is well said, "Before they get up, they do not know what they are going to say; when they are speaking, they do not know what they are saying; and when they have sat down, they do not know what they have said."—*Sir Winston Churchill*

Case Study of Robert

Robert applied for the post of corporate trainer, and was called for demonstration of his domain knowledge. He was given with a couple of topics to choose and come prepared after a week for delivering his presentation. He did intensive research about the topic from various sources including Google; prepared an article; and sent it for publication to an international journal. He was excited as the journal had agreed to publish the manuscript, and he was confident of delivering his presentation successfully.

On the D-day, Robert delivered presentation extempore on the chosen topic. He was confident that panel of judges would be pleased with his presentation. However, one of the panel members asked him the reasons for not using power point presentation. Robert replied that he was comfortable to deliver extempore. Subsequently as a selection procedure, the panel members gave him one more topic and asked him to prepare within ten minutes to deliver the presentation. Robert was confident of the topic, and he prepared bullet points on a rough sheet given to him; entered the room; and delivered the demonstration extempore. After the completion of demonstration, Robert was asked why he did not use cue cards during presentation. Robert replied that he was comfortable without cue cards and also he was confident of delivering the speech without any aids. He left the interview room and the panel of judges said that Robert would be informed about the outcome after a week. When the results came in, to his surprise, Robert was not selected for the post of corporate trainer. Robert asked the selection committee to inform the areas for improvement. The head of the panel members said that everything was fine but he did not deliver power point presentation in the first demonstration, and in the second demonstration he did not use cue cards.

From this case study, it is obvious that power point presentations and cue cards play a crucial role in delivering the content effectively. We will discuss them in this chapter which are useful not only to the trainers but also the teachers.

What are Cue Cards?

Cue cards are like hint cards, prompt cards, and direction cards that provide clues to the presenters or trainers or teachers at the time of presentations and speeches. Let us look at few of the definitions of cue cards from various sources.

"A card,[1] unseen by the audience, carrying dialogue, lyrics, etc. as an aid to a television performer."

A large card held out of the audience's sight, bearing words or dialogue in large letters as an aid for a speaker or actor chiefly in television broadcasting.

These cue cards are used by newsreaders in television and actors in film industry that is held out by someone who is not seen by the camera. Some people also call cue cards as idiot cards.

Cue cards[2] were originally "invented" when Barney McNulty, a CBS page and former military pilot, was asked to write ailing actor Edd Wynne's script lines on large sheets of paper to help him remember his script. Barney volunteered for this duty because his training as a pilot taught him to write quickly and clearly. Barney soon saw the necessity of this concept and formed the company "Ad Libs".

To overcome some of the shortcomings and also to improvise the cue cards Teleprompters came in where actors made use of it to deliver their dialogues. A teleprompter[3] is an electronic device used primarily to display text and cues for on-air newscasters and other professional talents. However, many of the teachers, trainers and presenters still use cue cards because of several advantages.

Merits of Cue Cards

Here are the merits of cue cards:

- Aids as a memory device to the presenter.
- Provides confidence and comfort to the presenter.
- Helps in staying focused on the key contents. It is human tendency to go off the track during the course of delivering speech. Cue cards check the presenter to be on the right track and on the smooth track.
- Minimizes human mistakes, which usually happen when depended on memory.
- Provides chronological and systematic approach to presentation.
- If there are any problems in verbal cues during presentation, the cue cards will set it alright.
- Helps in maintaining proper pauses during speech.
- Provides flexibility for the presenter by allowing both the presenter to speak and also the listeners to absorb and assimilate the contents smoothly and easily.
- It is rightly said that a picture is worth hundred words. The cue cards have tremendous effect on the minds of the audience.
- It eliminates usage of fillers like "um, ha, he, ok", etc.

Although there are plenty of merits in usage of cue cards, there are certain areas we must take certain precautions and the same is mentioned as follows:

Precautions

There are certain precautions to be observed while using cue cards. Write only one side of the cue cards and do not write on both sides as it will not have clarity, and also it diverts the attention of the audience. Excessive looking at the cue cards loses the eye contact with the audience leads to disconnection with audience. Ensure that the cue cards are short and precise. Ensure that there is a right coordination and synchronization between the cue cards and delivery of presentation. In this context, let us look at styles and types of presentations and the tools and techniques during presentation.

Types of Presentations

There are three kinds of presentations. They are impromptu presentation; prepared and read presentation; and the presentation in which there is conversation with the audience with cue cards. In case of impromptu presentation, the speaker emphasizes on memory which is often stressful. At times it loses its focus from the audience as the speaker concentrates on the memorized stuff. In the case of prepared and read presentation, although it is good, it may not be effective as it loses eye contact with the audience resulting in boredom and monotony. In the third type of presentation, the audience is very much actively involved in the presentation as there are cue cards, interaction, questioning, and participation. This is the best of all the three types of presentations.

Tips during Presentation

For any presentation to be successful, there are certain tools and techniques through which one can connect and impress the audience. Every presentation will have the introduction, body and summary. And the time allotted to the same can be; 10 per cent of time towards introduction, 80 per cent towards body and 10 per cent towards summary. The time mentioned is an indicator, and can be flexible depending on the topic and also on the profile of the audience. Having decided the time for each segment, let us know that there are always three segments among the audience. The first segment does not know anything about topic of the presentation, the second segment knows a little about the topic, and the third segment is expert on the topic. The introduction and the summary part is to be focused on the segments who do not know and who know a little on the topic, and the body of the presentation is to be focused on the segment who are experts on the topic. If this strategy is followed, the presentation will engage all segments of the audience equally.

Sergeant Major said, "Tell them what you are going to tell them, just tell them and tell them what you told them." This is about any type of presentation. At the introductory part, the presenter should tell the theme and idea or theme of the topic; at the body part, the presenter must highlight the theme, and at the end, the presenter must summarize what was presented succinctly. During presentation, the presenter should focus on three aspects such as the self, the content, and the audience. Usually, presenters fail in this area as few presenters are over sensitive about the audience forgetting about themselves, and on the content. Some presenters focus too much on content, not on audience and themselves. And few presenters focus on themselves forgetting on the audience and also the content. Therefore, the right presenter should focus on the audience, content and on self equally.

During presentation, the presenter should focus on the entire audience equally by maintaining eye contact with all. If the audience is huge, then it is advisable to fix one person in each side of the audience as a point, and shift his eyeball movement equally in different directions so that the audience feels that the presenter is talking to all. Never look at a particular individual for a longer duration as it causes discomfort to the individual. In a nutshell, never look at an individual for more than four seconds. The ideal focus on an individual should be between two to four seconds and then shift eyeball movement from one person to another. And also for presenters who are beginners, it is advisable to deliver one sentence by looking at one individual and another sentence with another person and so on. When it is practiced in this way, the presenters will gain confidence and become successful professional presenters. Finally, do not stand in one place while delivering the presentation. On the other hand, move freely in the room and deliver, as it looks lively, engaging, and interesting.

Stages of Cue Cards

There are three stages of cue cards such as making cue cards; preparing speech as per the cue cards; and writing and rehearsing cue cards. While making cue cards ensure that each idea is put in each card, the letters are bigger than the normal size, use only one side of the cue card for better clarity, number it chronologically, and finally, include emotions to make it effective and efficient. While preparing the speech for the cue cards ensure that the flow is logical, allocate time for structure and delivery of the contents and speak louder for your feedback. Taking feedback helps in checking your pitch levels at the time of presentation, and helps in delivering better presentation. While writing cue cards make sure that different colored cue cards are used for each activity such as for main idea one type of colored cue card; for supporting idea another colored cue card; for quotations another colored cue card; and for transition a separate colored cue card; and finally for summary a different colored cue card. Each color of cue card represents each stage of presentation. After having done entire work rehearse with cue cards for effective presentation.

Tips for Cue Cards

1. Keep number of points per slide between 4 to 5.
2. Keep cue cards in bullet format.
3. For better visibility of cue cards keep the font size large enough to enable the audience to see from distance and understand the contents.
4. Keep the background of the cue cards neutral.
5. Don't decorate cue cards.
6. Avoid adding uninteresting information.
7. And finally, make your flow natural from one cue card to another.

Action Exercises

Call two or three volunteers to come forward from the audience; ask them to name any one topic of their choice; give them white sheets to write the topic; and tell them to write the key points about their chosen topic. Let other members also watch, but they should not disclose the key points about the topic. Once the volunteers wrote the key points in skeleton format, ask other members (non-volunteers) among the audience to include few more key points on the same topic which are meaningful, and add value to the topic. And then ask them to rearrange the key points in a chronological order, and make a mnemonic device. Make it as precise as possible and it should work as a trigger to the mind of the presenter. Ask the volunteers to make cue cards from the key points.

If this exercise is done number to times, it helps the audience unlock their hidden creative ideas and encourage their thoughts chronologically, and helps in preparing cue cards effectively and efficiently.

To sum up, cue cards are the clue cards for both presenters and audience. Although the technology is changing rapidly and other electronic devices are inundated with much better benefits and advanced features than cue cards, the role of cue cards can neither be underestimated nor undermined in the years to come. We can therefore, conclude convincingly that cue cards are indeed the clue cards for any presentation to ensure effective takeaways for the audiences.

NOTES

1. http://www.yourdictionary.com/cue-card as accessed on 08 September 2008.
2. http://www.answers.com/topic/cue-card as accessed on 09 September 2008.
3. http://www.wisegeek.com/what-is-a-teleprompter.htm as accessed on 10 September 2008.

REFERENCES

http://professormsraoguru.blogspot.com

http://professormsrao.blogspot.com

http://profmsr.blogspot.com

http://www.yourdictionary.com/cue-card

http://www.answers.com/topic/cue-card

http://www.wisegeek.com/what-is-a-teleprompter.htm

7

Principals are Academic Leaders

> There will have to be rigid and iron discipline before we achieve anything great and enduring, and that discipline will not come by mere academic argument and appeal to reason and logic. Discipline is learnt in the school of adversity.—*Mahatma Gandhi*

Principals have a crucial role to play to enhance the quality of education, and to uplift the values of educational institutions. They have a number of challenges such as they must create compatibility between the teaching and non-teaching employees, maintain right synergy between the educators and the students and ensure coordination among the educators, and above all, they should be ready to provide academic leadership to their institutions through their knowledge, experience, impeccable integrity and honesty. All of them are easier said than done. Principal of an educational institution can be compared with the president of a nation who has to set an example to everyone by walking the talk. The people of the nation respect their president only when he or she delivers goods properly, and influences them through example. No amount of rhetoric will work when they don't set an example. Similarly, in educational institution the employees, educators, students and the board that appoints principal observes closely and keenly the every movement of the principal. Precisely, principal is constantly under the scanner of the all. Hence, principals have many challenges in setting an example, managing and leading the educational institution.

Robert Katz and Levels of Management

The principals must blend teaching, administration, management, curriculum development, and research to excel as true academic leaders. Robert Katz said that there are three skills needed at each level of management. They are technical skills, human skills, and conceptual skills. When someone joins as a faculty member he or she must possess more of technical skills and less of conceptual skills, and it falls under low level of management. After some experience, the faculty member must possess more of conceptual skills, and the emphasis on technical skills comes down gradually. The faculty member may be in the position of Head of the Department or a position equivalent to it as per the hierarchy of the education institution. Here the faculty member directly reports to the principal. This falls under middle level management. Finally, when the faculty member acquires enormous experience, gains knowledge about the management of the education institution, then the faculty member comes to the position of principal where he or she must demonstrate most of conceptual skills and least of technical skills as the faculty member teaches less and leads more. This falls in the category of top level management. In these three levels of management, the importance of technical skills decreases gradually and conceptual skills increases while the importance of human skills remain constant. Hence, there is a lot of transformation taking place from the position of freshly recruited faculty members to the position of principals over a period of time in an educational institution. The entire process can be compared with the transformation of a caterpillar to a beautiful butterfly. The process is painful but converts faculty members into successful principals of academic institutions, and finally as academic leaders.

My Experiences as a Principal

When I worked as the principal of a business school in India, I realized the roles and responsibilities of a principal and the challenges involved in it. Looking from outside is totally different than looking from within the role of principal. Keeping in view of Indian context, I had to balance both the promoters of the institution and the employees who treated me as their colleague, rather than as a principal. I was not in a position to antagonize the promoters who had very high expectations on me, and expected me to lead within the limited resources and with several constraints. And also, the teaching and non-teaching staff pinned tons of faith in my academic leadership and had very high expectations on me. Several issues surfaced during my tenure and I found it challenging to manage the pulls and pressures of promoters and teaching and non-teaching staff. Added to my woes were the grievances by students against few faculties due to their poor performance and improper interaction. I had to give constructive feedback to the educators without taking the names of students so that educators don't settle scores with students and, finally they live up to the expectations of students. Often I had to juggle from various roles and responsibilities as an educator, administrator, troubleshooter, and curriculum developer. At times, I felt upset as I did not get time to teach as teaching was close to my heart. And teaching requires a lot of preparation, and again it requires a lot of attention on my part. From my experience, I realized that the principal of an educational institution is sandwiched between the promoters on the one side, and the employees and the students on the other side. The role of principal requires a lot of balancing act depending on the priorities, situation and the type of academic institution the principal works.

Are Principals the Leaders?

There is no difference between the principals and the leaders as good leaders can only become good principals. Principals often juggle between several roles in educational institutions as administrators, managers, curriculum developers, academic builders and above all, academic leaders. It is indeed a very challenging task for them, but makes them great institution builders and leaders.

Principals have a huge responsibility where they have to ensure academic success and leadership without earning ill-will from others such as students, parents, educators, non-teaching employees, promoters of the institution and others. It is easier said than done as they cannot keep all sections in good humor. If they want to keep a particular section of people in good humor, others will be dissatisfied and, finally the effectiveness of the academic institution comes down which defeats the very purpose of being principals thus adversely affecting their prestige.

Principals must be visionaries who can take their institutions to greater heights of glory. They must play a crucial role in human resources by recruiting and developing them constantly. They must update themselves constantly that are happening in other educational institutions, and above all, they must learn to innovate their tools and techniques to stay ahead of others. Hence, principals must attend workshops to update and upgrade themselves from time to time. It helps them know what is happening around apart from networking and growing as academic leaders. In addition, they must reinvent themselves with the rapid changing times and technologies. They must come out of their comfort zones and constantly strive to stay in effective zones to lead academic institutions effectively. There is growing specialization, branding and changing needs and expectations of students globally. They must catch up with the pace, update, and upgrade themselves constantly to excel as academic leaders and to become role models for others thus making a difference in the lives of students.

REFERENCES

Author's Blogs:

http://professormsraoguru.blogspot.com

http://professormsrao.blogspot.com

http://profmsr.blogspot.com

PART II
Management Education

8

Challenges for Management Educators

> Teaching is the only major occupation of man for which we have not yet developed tools that make an average person capable of competence and performance. In teaching we rely on the "naturals," the ones who somehow know how to teach.—*Peter Drucker*

Local vs. Global Business Schools

The difference between the local business schools and the top business schools is that the local business schools explain various basic concepts, theories, the pros and cons, and the application of the topic vis-à-vis the corporate world. In contrast, the global business schools assume that the students are aware of these fundamentals and come out with case studies and encourage case study discussion in the classroom. The advantage with top business schools is that they get the best talent across the world where students bring in their knowledge, experience and network. When students with such profile participate in the classroom and discuss the case studies you can imagine the kind of value they add to classroom learning. When best brains discuss it is a great value addition for the students as there is more of collaboration in knowledge among the students. At the same time, the facilitators or the faculty members are highly experienced with excellent academic profile, and with industry, research, consultancy and training experience. They are highly focused on specialized areas and, therefore, they add immense value to case study discussion. During the case study discussion, the facilitators listen to all kinds of views, ideas and arguments and, finally, they unfurl their ideas, and conclude the case study discussion. In addition, most of the faculty from top business schools teach less and research more in their specialized areas and that make them stand out from their counterparts of local business schools. Here a question may arise among many people why such faculty and students are not available in local business schools. The answer is very simple—everything comes at a price. The global business schools collect a huge fee from students and maintain highest quality standards. Their academic ambience is unique and outstanding. They pay handsome salaries to faculty and provide faculty with more opportunities for career growth by encouraging research and consultancy. And the same is missing in local business schools due to lack of funds. However, there are always exceptions as there is a possibility of highly talented faculty members and students in local business schools also thus adding value to it.

Challenges for Management Educators

Currently, educators face several challenges in teaching. With easy access to information to students and information overload students demand more from educators and the latter find it tough to meet the rising aspirations and expectations of the former. The Internet has revolutionized the entire world and made the world a small village where everything has been thrown open with little secrecy for all of us. Here are the crucial challenges for educators globally:

Students have become smarter and sharper with availability of knowledge and information where students often fail to differentiate between information and knowledge. Educators must differentiate clearly that information is not knowledge and there is a thin line that separates them. They must also enlighten students to stay away from information overload as it clutters their minds leading to confusion. In addition, it wastes students' precious time.

Students expect a lot from educators and want something different from them. Hence, educators must do extensive research in their disciplines and create new concepts with case studies, examples and illustrations to stand out from others. In addition, they must also innovate new teaching tools and techniques as the traditional ones are losing their relevance. They must involve students into the teaching process by way of interacting, questioning and grilling thus pulling them out of their comfort zones. Encouraging students' participation in the teaching process is needed as it not only makes the teaching more effective but also brings benefits to both educators and students thus making it a win-win for all. A good educator is a good learner and s/he must learn from students. Peter Drucker said that he had learnt a lot from students when he shared his knowledge and experience with his EMBA students.

Finally, the educators have a great challenge where they have to meet the rising aspirations and expectations of students. It can happen only when educators teach with passion with complete command over their discipline. They must do continuous research and share their knowledge with students. While sharing their knowledge, the questions raised by students must be noted down and thoroughly researched. It helps them widen their knowledge base and stand firmly on their feet while teaching in the classroom apart from commanding respect from students. Hence, educators must not take their students for granted. They must come out of their comfort zones to know the pulse of their students and prepare themselves accordingly to stand out from others.

Professors and Their Teaching Styles in Business Schools

The faculty members in business schools must be a blend of academic, industry, research, and consultancy background so that the students are benefited from their diversified experiences. However, it is rare to find such breed of faculty in most of the business schools currently. In fact, teaching differs from professor to professor as no two professors are alike in knowledge, competencies, experiences, and passion. The professors who have only academic experience follow more of concepts and written case studies, and deliver their lectures based on theoretical knowledge. They are also more into syllabus- and examination-oriented. The professors who hail from industry background deliver sessions based on their industrial experience and connect students from classroom to corporate quickly. They relate reel content with real life experiences and events to ensure effective takeaways among the students. However, they may not focus much on theoretical concepts and aspects that are often emphasized by the professors hailing from pure academic background. At the same time, the professors who come from research background deliver their sessions based on latest developments on the subject thus adding value to the existing knowledge. They can deliver both theoretical and research perspective but often fail to connect students from classroom to corporate background as they don't have any industrial experience. Finally, the professors who come from consultancy and training background deliver teaching sessions based on their corporate and consultancy background but don't offer anything from theoretical perspective. Hence, teaching by the professors depends on their knowledge, experience, background and, above all, their passion to make a difference in the lives of students.

Students must note these facts and must not expect diversified knowledge on a platter from professors as each professor comes out with a particular knowledge, competence, and experience. Here is a great quote from Confucius, a Chinese philosopher: "A good student is someone who listens to what I say, adapting my teachings to his life, but never following it literally. It is someone who doesn't look for a job, but looks for work that dignifies him. And lastly, it isn't someone who seeks to be noticed, but someone who seeks to make something notable."

Are Educators the Facilitators?

> Education is not the filling of a pail but the lighting of a fire.—*William Butler Yeats*

Nowadays, tons of information is available on the Internet for both students and educators. Some students think that they are equally smart like educators due to the availability of online information. However, the fact is that the students often don't know the difference between the chalk and the cheese. They don't know the difference between information and knowledge. It is the educators, who read wide number of books, acquire information, do extensive research in the area, synthesize, structure, and finally, create and customize the content as per the profile of audiences, and deliver the same on a platter to the students in the classroom. In this regard, we will discuss the concept of 'Five Minds' coined by Howard Gardner, a noted psychologist from Harvard Business School.

Howard Gardner and Five Minds

> Education is a social process. Education is growth. Education is not a preparation for life; education is life itself.—*John Dewey*

Dr. Howard Gardner coined Five Minds and explains it as follows: The Five Minds are disciplined mind, synthetic mind, creative mind, respectful mind, and ethical mind. The disciplined mind helps create sustained focus in a specific area to have deeper understanding of the discipline. The synthetic mind effectively integrates various facets of the available information through thorough research thus creating meaningful and relevant knowledge for catering to students. The creative mind takes the available knowledge, and creates something new by adding value to what to the existing knowledge. The respective mind tolerates and empathizes with others and, especially, appreciates the differences of opinions and ideas of others. Finally, the ethical mind deals with higher level of abstraction and conceptualization. Dr. Gardner implores educators to keep all these Five Minds in their mind to ensure effective takeaways among the students.

Iyanla Vanzant remarked, "Education does not take place when you learn something you did not know before. Education is your ability to use what you have learned to be better today than you were yesterday." It is the educators who have to facilitate the learning. They should become facilitators rather than as educators. They must differentiate between information and knowledge. Whatever is available on the Internet may be information but may not be knowledge. They must convert the information into knowledge by going beyond books and sharing their experience, expertise, knowledge and synthesize the same and provide the essences on a platter to students. In addition, they must add value to what students already know to command respect, and to stand out.

Presently, educators face several challenges to stay ahead of others. Only the educators who are passionate and who have a vision to make a difference in the lives of students can stand out while the rest will fall flat. In addition, the expectations of the people are rising from all quarters. For instance, clients expect more from companies, employees expect more from employers, children expect more from parents and, finally, students expect more from educators. Hence, educators must pull up their socks, work hard, smart and wise to deliver their best to leave a mark behind for others to follow. Above all, they must become facilitators to ensure effective learning in the classrooms.

Good Educators Learn from Their Students

> I am here to teach you whatever I know and learn whatever you know.—*Professor M.S. Rao, Founder of MSR Leadership Consultants India*

Good teachers are great learners. They learn from all sources so as to teach effectively for their students. Ego doesn't prevent them learning from their students as well. These days students are much smarter than teachers as they think unconventionally, and handling such students has become a major challenge for teachers. Because of the exposure to technology and the availability of information at the click of mouse, students have accessibility to more information. As a result, their expectations have gone up. And they want more from their teachers. The conventional teachers read books, prepare teaching sessions and share their knowledge with students. Students don't appreciate such teachers currently as they expect more from teachers and that too beyond books. As a result, teachers must do extensive research and produce the material that is unknown to students so that they can stand firmly on their feet and command respect from students.

I had a student, Tony who attended my leadership training sessions. He was working at middle level management and joined EMBA course to hone his skills and abilities. He had lots of ideas and shared with me. I encouraged him to share such valuable information in the presence of other students in the classroom so that students are benefited from him. Since Tony hailed from a prestigious company with good amount of experience, he had his own anecdotes to share. He was excited with my encouragement and started sharing his experiences. The students started enjoying his experiences and anecdotes and I also encouraged other students to share their corporate experiences.

Currently, my students enjoy my teaching sessions as it has become interactive with experiences of other experienced students. Hence, teachers must encourage students to come forward, and share their ideas and insights as it builds leadership qualities among students and generates more knowledge. Above all, teachers must have an open mind to listen and learn from their students without false-ego for the overall benefit of students.

Dear Educators! What Got You Here Won't Get You There

> Learning is finding out what you already know, Doing is demonstrating that you know it, Teaching is reminding others that they know it as well as you do. We are all learners, doers, and teachers.—*Richard David Bach*

You can learn a lot while evaluating manuscripts of your students, especially from their knowledge and experience. I learn a lot from my students the way they demonstrate their knowledge, articulate their ideas and present case studies in the classroom. Few educators hesitate to learn from their students and are ashamed of admitting this fact. In some cases, ego prevents some educators learning from their students.

In fact, you can learn from various sources such as reading, observation, training, experience, practice and from your students as well. I teach the students of EMBA, and I am glad to share with you that I share a lot of knowledge with them. And also, I encourage interaction among my students during teaching sessions. Sometimes I am amazed the way the Gen Y demonstrates their ideas and knowledge. They are really superb! At times, I find their thought process is highly advanced, unique and unconventional. Their thoughts, ideas and insights add value to my teaching session. I also update my content at the end of each session by incorporating new things I learn from students and also do thorough research in those areas. The educators who take feedback constantly and learn from their students will be able to make a great contribution to teaching.

When I evaluate manuscripts of my EMBA students I read thoroughly to find out something new to add value to my teaching. I also give them constructive feedback and encourage them to do better. Do you find time to do that? If so, your success rate as an educator is higher. I am proud to declare that my students keep sending me emails as and when they achieve big in their lives and some students who are yet to achieve big still stay in touch me for my guidance and support. I also have a huge collection of email ids of all my students, for whom I conducted both teaching and training sessions.

Remember what Marshall Goldsmith said, *What Got You Here Won't Get You There*. Hence, educators must pull up their socks and stay in touch with their students and learn from them also to excel as successful educators. They must handhold their students and provide direction to them. What worked in the past might not work in the future. Hence, change your tools and techniques of both learning and teaching, and take feedback from their students constantly to make a difference in their lives.

REFERENCES

Author's Blogs:

http://professormsraoguru.blogspot.com

http://professormsrao.blogspot.com

http://profmsr.blogspot.com

9

Challenges for Students

> Indian youth are strikingly more optimistic about their own future and also about the future of society. The general picture in other countries is that young people tend to be personal optimists but societal pessimists.—*Mats Lindgren, CEO and founder of Kairos Future Group*[1]

Why Do You Need MBA?

When one of the richest persons in the world, Mr. Laxmi Niwas Mittal was asked if he had any regrets in life, he replied for not doing MBA. Although he acquired enormous wealth and achieved success by leading in the steel sector globally, he still has regret for not doing MBA.

MBA is one of the most sought-after qualifications in India. After the completion of the graduation, the students prefer to go for this qualification because it offers ample of career opportunities. The engineering graduates are also opting for this management qualification as it widens their mental faculties and ensures quick career growth. As a result, we find mushrooming business schools in India. In this context, we will discuss the importance of this qualification.

Engineers are technically competent in their domain and can excel as good engineers. But it takes them only in one direction. When they are armed with MBA qualification they can work as engineers and managers. Precisely, they turn out to be technocrats and full-fledged professionals. Acquiring management qualification will be a value addition to their careers. Besides, it inculcates entrepreneurial skills and enhances the ability to expand their imagination levels. It is not only the case of engineers but also people from other streams prefer to pursue this course. The advantage of management education is that any graduate can opt for this course, as it is basically management oriented with least technical orientation. This provides ample ammunition for any graduate to pursue this course. With the growing population and economy, there will be more industries, and as a result, there is more need for managers and leaders across the country.

Challenges for Youth

Indian youth currently encounter three challenges—lack of soft skills, entrepreneurial skills, and leadership skills. It is a cause for concern indeed! We do not have unemployment problem rather we have umemployability problem in India as after completion of their education students do not find themselves with requisite skills and abilities to match up with the industry demands, standards and expectations. We will discuss soft skills in this context.

Soft skills are the non-domain skills that include various skills like communication skills, presentation skills, team building skills, business grace, etiquette, and other skills about people. The people should know how to deal with their clients, customers, and suppliers, and should know how to behave with their subordinates, peers and superiors. People are good at their domain knowledge, i.e. the area in which they are qualified and that becomes the technical knowledge, which is also known as hard skills. It is rightly said people rise because of their hard skills but fall due to dearth of soft skills. The present Indian educational system encourages more on domain knowledge and less on non-domain knowledge resulting in unemployability.

Second problem for the youth is lack of encouragement towards entrepreneurial skills. Entrepreneurship is the process of setting up own business venture, which involves enormous risk. It is not a cakewalk. It requires tons of energy and efforts. It invites active involvement round the clock because it involves having a business idea, mobilizing resources, proper execution skills, and managing both internal and external forces and factors to pursue the passion of entrepreneurship.

Although Indian youth are interested in taking risk, their parents do not encourage them due to the challenges involved in entrepreneurship. The parents want their children to get secured jobs and earn a decent regular income. They also want their old age to be properly secured. In developed countries, there are social security measures where government takes care of their citizens in old age. There are old age homes, unemployment insurance, and so many protections as they have already developed. Since India is still a developing nation, we cannot afford to provide social security measures to the citizens. Therefore, it discourages entrepreneurship. In the past, Indian economy was mixed economy, and it did not encourage entrepreneurship skills. Ever since the opening up of Indian economy the climate has become conducive for encouraging entrepreneurship among Indian youth.

The third problem for the Indian youth is lack of leadership qualities. India with a 1.3 billion plus population doesn't have proportional representation of leaders globally. Although you cannot have leaders as per the size of population, there is a cause for concern due to lack of enough leaders in India. In fact, we don't have the right ambience to learn, explore and experiment leadership. Greg Chappel, former Indian Cricket Coach opined, "The Indian culture is very different, it's not a team culture. They lack leaders in the team because they are not trained to be leaders. From an early age, their parents make all the decisions, their school teachers make their decisions, and their cricket coaches make the decisions." He further adds, "The culture of India is off. So they learn to keep their head down and not take responsibility. The Poms (British) taught them really well to keep their head down. For if someone was deemed to be responsible, they'd get punished. So the Indians have learned to avoid responsibility." In fact, leadership is the ability to inspire others, and it is having a fire in the belly to achieve something unimaginable. It is like having self-motivation to push ahead despite stiff opposition. It is like having an extra spark.

The present educational and economic environment is not encouraging the leadership qualities. In some cases, there is a dearth of talent. And in some cases, there is talent but it is not being adequately tapped to develop as leaders. We do not have adequate training institutes that encourage and develop skills.

Industry Expectations

Industry looks for plug and play recruits. They want the recruited employees to be on their toes right from the day one. They want the freshers to be industry ready so that they can be productive and useful. However, it is not the scenario. Lot of jobs are available and the industry is not getting the competent manpower to execute the tasks. There are a set of skills that the industry expects from the freshers. They are learnabilty—the ability and capability to learn new tools and techniques, absorbability—the ability to grasp and understand new kind of tasks, suitability—looking for the right peg in right hole. Nobody likes to have a round peg in a square hole or a square peg in a round hole. Capability—the ability to execute the challenging tasks at ease is another trait expected from the industry. And skills like adaptability, flexibility, assertiveness, team spirit, communication, leadership skills, and last but not least is the passion to learn and grow. To put it succinctly, they look for right mindset, tool set, and skill set.

Infosys, the Indian IT giant started a programme titled 'Campus Connect' where the faculties of various institutions are selected and called for Soft Skills Workshops. It is a kind of Corporate Social Responsibility. The faculties are trained free of cost who in turn train the faculties in their respective institutions. And the faculties provide training to the students in soft skills and other skills that are needed for the students to get placed in the industry. Likewise, many IT companies are taking initiative in this regard. It is an indication that everyone is realizing the importance of employability skills, and its results will be felt in the near future. It is like a ripple effect.

Challenges

Students work hard and climb the ladder to reach the heights of success and then they realize that the ladder is on the wrong side of the wall. It indicates that youth lack right direction, guidance and counseling. In fact, problem lies with their wrong selection of career goals and objectives. They set the goals because of parental or peer influence, or sometimes because of herd instinct. In the long run, it does not give any satisfaction resulting in frustration and fatigue. While planning their career the youth should look for 4As—Aptitude, Attitude, Abilities and Awareness. When their career is planned in this way, they can easily accomplish their goals and career aspirations.

Because of growing technology, the business environment has become highly challenging, and as a result, the employees have to deliver their best to meet the rising demands of the customers and consumers. During this process, if any employee falls short of expectations, he will be served with pink slips. There is more element of risk involved even in employment. The youth should learn to perform well or else they will perish. It is a case of 'do or die' situation where non-performing and inefficient employees are shown the door. There is more need for smart work rather than hard work.

Leaders and Managers

> Management is doing things right; leadership is doing the right things.—*Peter Drucker*[2]

There is a vast difference between the leaders and the managers. Let us look at the difference between the leaders and the managers. Managers are efficient while leaders are effective. Managers climb the ladder whereas the leaders place the ladder on the right side of the wall. Managers are missionaries while the leaders are visionaries. Leaders know what to do whereas managers know how to do. Managers put in hard work whereas leaders put in smart work. Succinctly, if managers are the actors, the leaders are the directors. However, in the recent past there is a growing emphasis on managerial leaders which is a combination of managerial and leadership qualities and, of course, the combination of hard work and smart work.

Overseas Indians

Indians are doing extraordinarily well overseas because of various reasons. Laxmi Niwas Mittal did amazingly well as an entrepreneur thus becoming one of the top ten richest persons in the world. Indra Nooyi, PepsiCo chief is one of the most powerful women in the world who is a symbol of success and a guiding and motivating model for Indian women. All these people could do it because of several reasons such as more opportunities in overseas and also probably they shift from comfort zone to effective zone. Renowned Motivational Guru, Zig Zigler Zig said, "97 per cent of the people live in comfort zone and only 3 per cent of the people live in effective zone". And success comes to the people who live in their effective zones. The successful people keep shifting their orbits and reinvent themselves as per the changing conditions and scenario. To sum up, Indian youth must overcome challenges to be competitive and must also pursue management education to avail number of opportunities.

NOTES

1. http://www.forbes.com/2007/09/22/india-happiness-survey-face-cx_rd_0921autofacescan02.html as accessed on 20 September 2008.
2. http://en.wikipedia.org/wiki/Peter_Drucker as accessed on 19 September 2008.

REFERENCES

Author's Blogs:

http://professormsraoguru.blogspot.com

http://professormsrao.blogspot.com

http://profmsr.blogspot.com

http://www.forbes.com/2007/09/22/india-happiness-survey-face-cx_rd_0921autofacescan02.html

http://en.wikipedia.org/wiki/Peter_Drucker

10

An Ideal Business School Student

> The function of the university is not simply to teach bread winning, or to furnish teachers for the public schools or to be a centre of polite society; it is, above all, to be the organ of that fine adjustment between life and the growing knowledge of life, an adjustment which forms the secret of civilization.—*W.E.B. Du Bois*

With the recent global meltdown, many doubts have been raised about the falling ethical and moral standards within the management education system. We cannot blame that the business schools and the students alone are responsible for the present economic crisis. However, we need to set certain standards and benchmarks for the students to enable them avert such economic crises in future and become role models for others.

Qualities of an Ideal B-School Student

Management students should be equipped with knowledge about management in general with special emphasis on a particular functional skill. It is vital to know the basic jargon about management, how a company is run and what it takes a company successful. They should know about various skills including soft skills and hard skills. They should learn to live with uncertainty and complexity which are the hallmarks in this century.

An ideal B-school student should possess several skills such as hard skills, soft skills like communication skills, interpersonal skills, entrepreneurial skills, leadership skills, team building skills, presentation skills, conceptual, critical and analytical thinking skills, business skills, conflict management skills, decision-making skills, visioning skills, risk taking skills, right attitude and aptitude, ethical and moral values, and learn to live with uncertainty and complexity.

How should the Teaching Process Be?

Explain the concept clearly from book as knowledge about the managerial jargon is necessary. Follow the concept with a relevant case study based on real life events and experiences. Ask the students how can they handle such problems through interactions? Generate multiple ideas and insights through interaction and participation and select the best, and justify the same by focusing the pros and cons. Then take the students to the corporate houses and encourage them to apply what has been learnt in the classroom to build confidence.

Brainstorming sessions among students and also between faculties and students excite the teaching process resulting in generation of multiple ideas and insights. The gap between the faculties and the students should be minimized to make the learning process more comfortable and meaningful. Assimilation of others' approaches makes the teaching more meaningful and effective.

Faculty should come out with their own philosophies and principles apart from the established and proven ones. They should equip their students with tools and techniques so that they could employ the same in their organizations. The curriculum should help in thinking differently. It should encourage to think globally but to act locally. There should be right mechanism and quality controls in the method of teaching.

Evaluating Students

The present examination system is outdated and needs to be reviewed and changed with the changing times. Give practical problems to students and encourage them to think and come out with their solutions. Students should be encouraged to prepare their own case studies based on their imagination after referring several books and industry interface. This method unlocks their creativity and originality which in turn helps them when they face the real challenges.

Bridge the Gap between the Campus and the Industry

There is a vast gap between the campus and the industry. The business schools don't teach skills like risk taking, entrepreneurial skills, facing failures, managing uncertainty and complexity. There are a number of areas where the business schools should focus and teach students. The main challenge for business schools is to teach how to cope up with failures and how to pick up threads again and bounce back from failures. We will discuss them elaborately in the next chapter.

An ideal B-school student should be jack of all trades and master of a specific subject. Mere having domain expertise is not adequate. There has to be focus on ethical and moral values among the students to eliminate white collar crimes. S/he should be person with impeccable character and integrity so that the subordinates can take as a role model. S/he should not sell soul for the sake of money.

An ideal B-school student should think globally and act locally and should be blend of both managerial and leadership qualities. To sum up, the faculties, the business schools and parents have a crucial role in shaping ideal B-school students.

REFERENCES

Author's Blogs:

http://professormsraoguru.blogspot.com

http://professormsrao.blogspot.com

http://profmsr.blogspot.com

11

What They don't Teach in Business Schools?

> We can teach a lot of things, but if the teacher can't relate by talking to a group of friendly students, he'll never be a competent teacher.—*William Glasser*

Although India has a good number of business schools, it could not produce the best business leaders and managers across the world. We often glorify about our quantity of management students and education, not the quality. In this chapter, we will discuss what is not taught in business schools as it helps ensure quality management education.

Business Schools in India

What makes students crazy after MBA tag? Is it because MBA degree offers wider career opportunities with good a compensation package? It is a debatable issue indeed! Especially after the opening up of Indian economy in early nineties, many private players jumped into the bandwagon of establishing B schools with money spinning attitude. It is very difficult to predict how many institutions will survive and succeed, and how many will vanish. The institutions are in a great hurry to create managers in quantity, not in quality.

Students find it fancy to go for such courses to suffix their names with MBA, to have wider career opportunities and brand themselves as management graduates.

The MBA degree is the brainchild of American educational system, and in early fifties in the last century Indian Institute of

Management (IIM) has been established in India to provide management education. Since then IIMs have become the official, authoritative and commendable institutions in India. The present Indian business education system is American in content, context, and nature resulting in critical gaps in the Indian business education system.

Management Education for Non-Professional Degrees Holders

In India, there is a strong need to encourage students of Arts, Commerce, Science, and Computer to go for MBA courses. Also inclusion of management subjects or topics or concepts in these areas will enhance their exposure to the field of management so that they can develop an aptitude for management. When these degree holders from non-professional background go for placement they find themselves fully equipped to face the day-to-day challenges in their workplace. In fact, the strength of non-technical graduates outnumbers technical graduates. As a result, there will be steady and strong growth of appetite for MBA qualification. Ultimately, we can expect more number of managers from all streams.

Weaknesses in the Present Management Education

Henry Mintzberg is one of the strongest critics of MBA degrees. He found several drawbacks in the present management education system. The present system does not encourage entrepreneurial skills and abilities. It does not stress on ethical part of education. It is not able to inculcate or cultivate industry or sector specific skills. In fact, there are set of skills required for each sector, segment, and industry. The inability to focus on the same has become a major area of weakness. Real industrial problems are neither thought nor taught. It is not able to cater to Indian type of education. On the contrary, it aped the American method of education, which at times found to be highly irrelevant and superfluous. It is devoid of multicultural experience. It is highly commercialized and commoditised. It is like a shop where goods and services are offered in exchange for money. Of course, no qualifications can be provided without money, as money is essential to ensure circulation of the entire organizational set up effectively. The degree of commercialization and commoditisation has become rampant. It is filled with antiquated, outdated and condemned pedagogic and teaching skills, and needs to be overhauled immediately.

Strengths

The present management education survived for more than six decades in India and is struggling to expand beyond national and geographical boundaries. With the boon of rapid changing technology and communication, the educational system is undergoing drastic changes although the pace is slow. The students in B-schools develop the ability to network and grow fast. The alumni links serve as strong launching pad.

What They don't Teach in B-Schools?

B-schools teach the theoretical concepts and aspects, which help students to get tuned with the corporate terminology right from the school itself. The tools and techniques taught in school help them to be equipped to take over the managerial/leadership roles in the corporate world. In fact, B-schools' objective is to groom the business leaders for tomorrow. But the outcomes are opposite as there is vast chasm between theory and practice. The B-school product finds himself/herself suffocated as s/he finds vast gap in his/her dreams and realities. S/he needs to get his/her hands dirty in the real organizations, which s/he might have fantasized, from a totally different perspective when s/he was in B-school.

The ability to deal with the people cannot be taught in B-schools and even if it is taught, it is very difficult to implement, as there will be so many bottlenecks. B-schools only teach how to do but the corporate world teaches the practical way of learning. It is like learning how to swim, i.e. whatever the student learned such as tools and techniques by way of theoretical explanations in school, he can only learn when he gets into the deep waters of the corporate world.

Traits like diplomacy and tactness and emotional intelligence can be learnt only from practical experience. The books and B-schools have certain limitations. The efficiency and efficacy can be learnt only by involving oneself in real life situations.

The concepts like brainstorming, reverse brainstorming, lateral thinking, vertical thinking, out-of-the-box thinking, emotional intelligence, change agents, mind mapping, morphological analysis, six thinking hats, synectics, Type A and Type B personality to name a few could be better be understood and felt in the real corporate life.

B-schools equip tons of information, data, knowledge, and case studies, which can help to get tuned with the real problems in the organizations to some extent. But it cannot be summed up altogether that they produce the best managers in the industry.

B-schools do not teach entrepreneurial skills and risk taking abilities. They teach soft skills and communication skills, which can best be experimented and perfected in the battleground of corporate world. If the tools of efficiency are taught in B-schools, the tricks of effectiveness are learnt in corporate world.

B-schools do not talk much about building relations. Whatever the little so taught becomes too little in the practical life. In real business, it is always the products or services, which speak in volumes to the customers initially and the subsequent transactions, depend on relationships to a greater extent. Ultimately, it is the satisfied customer who comes back and gives business. Therefore, much of the business solely depends on building relationships, which is again missing in B-schools. B-schools do highlight on evolutionary approaches, not revolutionary approaches. But the practical business mostly talks of revolutionary approaches.

To go further, if 'what B-school teaches' is one side of the coin then the other side of the coin is 'what one learns in organizations'. And the coin will have complete value only when these two are clubbed together. The combination of two sides creates a complete corporate personality.

Filling the Critical Gaps

There is a strong need to emphasize on the Indian industry-oriented management education. This does not mean to do away with the American methodology of concepts and teachings. What is now needed is glocal approach, i.e. the combination of global and local approach.

The visiting faculty usually teaches in more than one institution and teaches more than one subject. As a result, their approach is short-term oriented and less focussed. Whereas the permanent faculty works under one roof in the same system and subjects resulting in staying highly focused in his/her approach. The permanent faculty tends to have long-term orientation, and it pays off heavily for the students.

There is a vast chasm between the salaries of academic and non-academic professions. The best brains opt for non-academic careers due to heavy pay and perks. This does not mean totally that those who work in academic profession do not possess great talents and skills. There may be a segment of brains that prefer to work in academia because of their taste for teaching. The vast gap between these two in terms of salaries needs to be narrowed down and addressed. Sometimes, the teaching faculty may work outside on part-time basis to generate more income.

Recruiting the faculty who possess diversified academic background, experience, and expertise will enhance quality of education as such faculty can combine their multiple skills learned from multiple backgrounds. Similarly, industries must come forward to encourage the trainee management graduates to do project work in their organizations which will enhance competency and confidence.

The present management education refers to many case studies from other countries. Although it is good to have a feel of the case studies of foreign land, there is an element of nativity lost in teaching. It is necessary to generate our own case studies and explain the concepts or topics with native examples for understanding and enhancing the qualitative education. The need of the hour is to create glocal mindset in the minds of management graduates.

Indian B-schools must evolve its own teaching tools and techniques and turn its B-schools as the battlegrounds to create global management gurus.

All India Council for Technical Education (AICTE) has a pivotal role to play in streamlining and overhauling Indian management education system with many checks and balances. Late Dhirubhai H. Ambani and Laxmi Niwas Mittal have become corporate legends not by doing MBA but by their business acumen and right application of available resources. MBA helps in enriching the minds of the business managers and leaders. Sound academic background with strong business and industry insights along with stimulated and simulated case studies can bring out the best results in entrepreneurs in India.

The best business managers and leaders can be created only by a successful synthesis of academic theory and business practices with industrial experience. The business education should be based on practical or simulated and effective case studies. If the educational infrastructure is sound, one can expect a strong superstructure in future. Hence, Business schools must address the challenges and provide practical education to prepare students to take on the corporate battles successfully.

REFERENCES

Author's Blogs:

http://professormsraoguru.blogspot.com

http://professormsrao.blogspot.com

http://profmsr.blogspot.com

12

Is Doctoral Degree a Decoration or a Qualification?

> The average Ph.D. thesis is nothing but a transference of bones from one graveyard to another.—*James Frank Dobie*

There is a heated debate within the academia about doctoral degree (PhD) whether it is a qualification or a mere decoration. Nowadays, AICTE in India has made PhD mandatory for acquiring professorship in educational institutions. In addition, PhD is an imperative to hold directorial and principal positions. It has become a thorny issue for the faculty members who hail from industrial and corporate background as most of them don't possess PhD. However, they have rich corporate experience under their belt. As they are beset with their corporate pressures they don't find academic ambience to pursue doctoral degree. In contrast, academicians who want to grow in academia pursue PhD comfortably as they are already in academic ambience. However, they don't have corporate experience. Those who have passion to teaching give up their lucrative corporate careers and join academics. Unfortunately, they are relegated to background in academia as they don't have PhD despite having vast industrial experience and practical exposure.

Hence, those who want to progress in academia are compelled to pursue PhD. And pursuing PhD is not an easy thing. There are so many challenges in pursuing PhD. I have seen few people who are highly capable with industrial experience leaving PhD in the initial stage itself due to non-cooperation from their guides who are highly egoistic academicians.

Few mischievous guides in India exploit research scholars in the name of research. They deliberately delay the research process to draw more attention from their research scholars or seek some favors. Having fed up with mischievous research guides few research scholars have given up pursuing PhD forever. It is also observed that there are PhD holders who don't have any academic stamina but bag doctoral degrees by manipulations. These days AICTE has made PhD mandatory for becoming professors and directors. Previously, people with considerable industry background enjoyed the status of professorship. However, the recent tightening of noose by AICTE to possess PhD for becoming professors forced educators from industry background behind in academia.

Some of the research scholars help pile up their guides' resumes with their publications. Some of the research scholars shell out their personal money to meet their guides' miscellaneous expenses. Some guides compel their research scholars to spend money when they go for paper presentations. If research scholars don't spend money, their PhD will be delayed. Few unscrupulous guides in India have vitiated research and academic ambience for their selfish gains.

For few academicians who regularly sharpen their saws doing research for PhD and post doctoral degree (PDC) is a passion. Such passionate academicians feel let down by unscrupulous guides who claim to the super persons with big egos and who have the habit of disagreeing what is produced and created by the research scholars.

I have seen few experts in academia having passion to acquire PhD and ultimately ended up without PhD due to such unscrupulous guides. Few guides think themselves as demigods and treat their research scholars with sadism thus leaving bad impression among the ambitious research scholars who have passion to make a difference in research, and acquire PhD.

Unlike other post graduate qualifications that can be acquired through examinations where the evaluators don't know who the examinees are, PhD is the one that has to be done with the supervision of guides. As a result, completion of PhD is in the sole hands of guide.

I have seen a woman faculty with strong academic credentials who was awarded as the best teacher from prestigious educational institution pursuing her PhD in Indian education. The guide deliberately sent the thesis to a foreign country for its evaluation and almost after a year the evaluators returned with comments that they are not experts in Indian education and commented that they will not evaluate the PhD thesis. The woman faculty was upset the way the guide deliberately did in this way thus delaying her PhD. She would have acquired PhD within four years, and now it is almost seven years, and is still struggling with her PhD with her guide who happens to be a woman.

Few guides trouble their research scholars when the latter don't meet their personal demands and expectations. Sometimes it could be money or writing papers for guides so that guides can publish on their names and take credit for publications.

If you want to grow academically you must possess PhD in most of the countries. Possessing PhD helps in widening your research skills thus becoming a successful academician. However, the road to acquisition of PhD is a tough task with several challenges for research scholars especially in a country like India.

To conclude, acquisition of doctoral degree has become a decoration for industry experts, a qualification for academicians, and a paper degree for passionate researchers in India.

REFERENCES

Author's Blogs:

http://professormsraoguru.blogspot.com

http://professormsrao.blogspot.com

http://profmsr.blogspot.com

PART III
Success

13

Managing People During Failures and Success

> It's fine to celebrate success but it is more important to heed the lessons of failure.—*Bill Gates*

When things are going good anybody can lead successfully. When the ship is sailing smoothly any captain can sail it successfully. However, when faced with storm, the real captains come to the fore to steer the ship successfully to the shore.

There are leaders who proved their leadership abilities when things were going good. However, they failed miserably when things went awry thus hitting rock bottom. When we look at leaders like Abraham Lincoln, he was an amazing example of taking the leadership baton when America was passing through a major crisis of North versus South and sailing smoothly by demonstrating extraordinary leadership qualities and maintaining the unity of America. He also handled the issue of slavery, and played a crucial role for its abolition.

When political leaders remain in opposition, it is tough to maintain their flock together as the ruling party attracts the key people from opposition to break the ranks and join the ruling political parties. The political leaders need to demonstrate their true leadership skills and constantly motivate their cadre to stay disciplined. They must raise hope among their party people for staging back to power. Of course, it is easier said than done to retain flock intact especially when the political parties are in opposition.

There will be a section of people who will also demotivate the people when the political party in opposition. Besides, problems come in battalions during failures. The leaders must spot such people and show the door as they spoil the rest of the people. They must continuously motivate themselves as well as their flock during failures to ensure victory finally. In fact, tough times are great times to learn lessons for leaders and to bring out the best in them. Hence, leaders must be careful during failures to charge up themselves constantly, and also their followers to achieve success finally.

Managing Success is More Challenging than Managing Failures

> Success is to be measured not so much by the position that one has reached in life as by the obstacles which he has overcome while trying to succeed.—*Booker T. Washington*

Managing success is more challenging than managing failures. It sounds strange right! Yes, when you achieve success more people flock around you to congratulate, and share your success. And you find it tough to manage them. At the same time you will have more challenges as there will be people who are envious of your success and criticize you by highlighting your weaknesses, negative past or sometimes criticize your means and methods of reaching to the top.

It is tough to recognize your real friends especially after achieving success. When you fail you can easily assess your friends who stand by you. It is true that prosperity brings friends while adversity tests them.

After achieving success, if you don't pay attention to others due to your busy schedules, you will be misunderstood that success has gone to your head. If you closely associate with everybody, few people may take undue advantage out of your closeness. They may send wrong signals to others. Sometimes people try to attack you to get noticed easily by others. These days, several small people with little egos began attacking the big leaders with shoes. Sometimes they slap the top people in public to get instant publicity. Therefore, the successful people must be more careful in protecting their image and managing their success. They know how hard to achieve success and they must also learn that maintaining success and retaining fame is still harder.

Hence, understand the intricacies involved in achieving success. Learn to manage your success well through proper time management. And above all, have humility to grow still taller in stature. Accept the reality that it is easy to manage failures but tough to manage your success.

REFERENCES

Author's Blogs:

http://professormsraoguru.blogspot.com

http://professormsrao.blogspot.com

http://profmsr.blogspot.com

14

Manage Multiple Channels and Make Your Decisions Wisely

> You can be anything you want to be, if only you believe with sufficient conviction and act in accordance with your faith; for whatever the mind can conceive and believe, the mind can achieve.—*Napoleon Hill*

The life has become highly complex. There is all round ambiguity. Managing time has become a huge challenge. The fact is that time management is a misnomer. However, there are tools and techniques if you follow you can manage time, complexity and ambiguity.

We all have inner dialogue that sets into motion the moment we wake up from bed to until we go to bed. That is very powerful and works constantly and continuously during the waking hours. If we make it positive, we can derive pleasure and positive results. In contrast, if we make it negative, we get pressure and negative results. It is also known as self-talk. First thing to be effective and productive in your life is to set your self-talk or inner dialogue positive as it sends healthy signals from your mind resulting in healthy body actions. It finally contributes to positive outcomes in your life.

Zig Ziglar once said, "If you want to reach a goal, you must 'see the reaching' in your own mind before you actually arrive at your goal." Hence, to be successful in this current cut-throat competitive world you can make use of your inner dialogue effectively. Engage your mind with multiple tasks simultaneously. That means you need to mentally plan multiple activities within your mind, and set them into motion. Ensure that the multiple activities gain adequate momentum. Keep focusing on them. Often, it happens that some activities derail due to external forces and factors. It is quite common and natural. Make it a point to ensure that the particular task is set into motion again by analyzing the reasons and addressing the same adequately and immediately. Once you have set all activities mentally into momentum, include few more activities within your mind and see that they keep moving forward. Likewise, you need to move and manage the things and activities within your mind constantly to achieve optimum outcome. If you want to achieve success in real life, you need to achieve success in your reel life. That means you need to win your mind with visualization so that you can achieve success in reality.

Charles Darwin rightly said, "It is not the strongest of the species that survives, nor the most intelligent that survives. It is the one that is the most adaptable to change." We need to change with the changing times and technologies to be successful in this complex and ambiguous world. Therefore, learn to adapt and learn to live with realities by setting your reel life with positive and healthy thoughts. Move and manage the multiple channels in your mind simultaneously to achieve all round success in your real life. Remember the words of Dr. Wayne W. Dyer: "The state of your life is nothing more than a reflection of your state of mind."

Go by Your Head, Heart or Gut

> Checking the results of a decision against its expectations shows executives what their strengths are, where they need to improve, and where they lack knowledge or information.—*Peter Drucker*

We all make decisions in our daily lives. Sometimes we curse ourselves for making wrong decisions. We want all our decisions must be successful. The fact is that all decisions that we make may not turn out to be fruitful as some of them end up in failures. Therefore, we will briefly discuss decision-making in this regard.

We make decisions based on our knowledge, the availability of information, prevailing circumstances, and based on head, heart and gut. Sometimes we make a decision and act and the very next moment we think that we have made a wrong decision as the mind changes fast. When we change our minds so rapidly and feel within ourselves that we have made a wrong decision then how can we blame others for making wrong decisions? The truth is that everybody wants their decisions must go right as nobody wants to make wrong decisions deliberately.

There are people who make decisions based on their head. That means through their analysis and logical thinking. There are people who make decisions based on their heart. That means based on their emotions, egos and feelings. There are people who make decisions based on their gut. That means through their intuition. In fact, decision-making is situational, and is based on knowledge, availability of information, personality of the individuals, and the prevailing circumstances. When you love someone you make decisions based on your heart as love is something related to your heart. When something related to your life you make decisions based on your head as you view various pros and cons about it. When you don't know what to do, you make decisions based on your gut. Therefore, decision-making is situational, and is based on various factors and forces.

Remember there is no magic wand to ensure the success of all decisions. Hereafter, don't regret for making wrong decisions as all decisions will not go right. At the same time, learn lessons from wrong decisions and move forward with takeaways. To conclude, think various aspects, weigh all options and blend your head, heart and gut and take a call to achieve all round success in your life.

Best of luck for better decision-making!

REFERENCES

Author's Blogs:

http://professormsraoguru.blogspot.com

http://professormsrao.blogspot.com

http://profmsr.blogspot.com

15

Sharpen Your Saw

> Knowledge has to be improved, challenged, and increased constantly, or it vanishes.—*Peter Drucker*

Currently, knowledge management is the buzzword in the corporate world. Companies proudly talk about it. Is it related to management of knowledge or something else? Let us find out the same.

According to Andersen Consulting, knowledge management (KM) is the systematic process of acquiring, creating, capturing, synthesizing, learning and using information, insights and experiences to enable performance. It converts ideas into realities. It helps in promoting the learning curve of their employees and retaining the same for the overall prosperity and progress of the organization.

KM is interwoven with information dissemination and information action. It is linked with talent management. Constant creativity and innovation are the pillars for knowledge management. Nowadays, the companies focus on managing and expanding their knowledge capital base in order to stay ahead of their counterparts competitively. It adds value to their organizations. However, very few companies hoard their knowledge and don't believe in sharing due to the fear of their employees being poached by competitors. In such a scenario, the company may not encourage their employees to grow intellectually resulting in stagnation.

KM promotes, furthers, nurtures knowledge in the organization, and ensures that the knowledge is managed within the company even in the event of the exit of the employees. KM highlights on collective knowledge of the enterprise through collaborative teamwork, knowledge sharing and mentoring.

The companies should provide conducive organizational culture and climate to ensure that knowledge is managed effectively and efficiently. Employees should equally actively involve in the successful sharing of knowledge. At times because of competition a few employees do not share their knowledge and retain within themselves.

It is observed that knowledge sharing is widely honoured while the knowledge hoarding is highly dishonoured. The companies should use knowledge management wholeheartedly not only for their survival and success but also to ensure the all-round development of their precious human resources. It is rightly said that knowledge grows when shared. Here is a great quote from Henry Ford: "If money is your hope for independence you will never have it. The only real security that a man will have in this world is a reserve of knowledge, experience, and ability."

Blend Business and Social Acumen

> Pleasure is a shadow, wealth is vanity, and power is a pageant; but knowledge is ecstatic in enjoyment, perennial in frame, unlimited in space and infinite in duration.—*DeWitt Clinton*

Nowadays, executives need both business acumen and social acumen. It sounds strange for executives as most of them think that business acumen is needed only for entrepreneurs. Of course, they are right to think in that way. However, for the executives who intend to reach top positions within the organizations quickly they must acquire business acumen and blend it with social acumen proportionately.

The literal meaning of the word 'acumen' is "keenness and depth of perception, especially in practical matters." Hence, we can define business acumen as seeing the big picture by entrepreneurs and leaders. It is a rare quality that can be cultivated by people. Similarly, social acumen is about gelling well with others through emotional intelligence and soft skills, and networking with others.

Ram Charan says in *Leaders at All Levels*, "Leaders must possess both people acumen and business acumen. Anyone can improve his or her ability to select and develop people's talents, but other aspects of people acumen are hard to teach. Leaders with people acumen have good instincts to anticipate problems among individuals who must work together and to get the resolved. When leaders are unable to make good decisions or any decisions at all, it may be that their business acumen is not expanding. They cannot be considered to have CEO potential." Therefore, blend both business and social acumen proportionately to acquire knowledge and ensure your professional success.

Sharpen Your Saw

> As long as you love and learn, you are young. The day you stop loving and learning you become old.—*Professor M.S. Rao, Founder, MSR Leadership Consultants, India*

Students often think that they can say "good bye" to education once they switch from academic life to corporate life. But the fact is that the real learning starts from corporate world. Whatever students have learnt academically puts them on the corporate ladder. However, in order to survive in the corporate world, they must work smart to acquire and hone new skills and abilities. Besides, they must also sharpen their saws continuously to race ahead of others.

Marshall Goldsmith in his book, *What Got You Here Won't Get You There How Successful People Become Even More Successful*, emphasizes on sharpening saws. People often get complacent with success and don't improve within the organizations. It proves costly in later part of their lives as their peers and subordinates will outsmart them professionally. What worked to reach the present position may not work to reach their next higher positions. Hence, there is a constant need to improve and grow in this world. In addition, Stephen R. Covey emphasizes sharpening saw in his book, *The Seven Habits of Highly Effective People*. The successful people have the habit of sharpening their saws constantly. They learn and grow continuously.

Improvement is important, and is an essential ingredient for all individuals. They must improvise, innovate and invigorate constantly to sharpen their saws. Here are the tools to sharpen your saws:

- Have an appetite for learning. Learn from everyone without any false-ego.
- Invest a part of your earnings for learning and development.
- Invest your time regularly for reading. As you take food for your sustenance, you must read daily to update and upgrade yourself.
- Learn from mistakes. We all make mistakes. But recognizing and realizing mistakes help us prevent mistakes in future to enhance our success rate.
- Strive for excellence, not perfection as perfection is mere impossible. Striving to be at your best gives you great satisfaction and motivates you to move forward.
- Above all, share your knowledge as knowledge grows when shared. The more you share, the more pleasure you derive out of it. You will be happy to see people growing in front of you with your knowledge.

Alvin Toffler said, "The illiterates of the 21st century are the people who cannot unlearn, relearn and learn." The rapid growth in technology has compelled people to perform. If people don't perform they will perish. There is no meaning to life if there is no continuous value addition. Hence, learn from everybody and from all sources to stay healthy stand out.

REFERENCES

Author's Blogs:

http://professormsraoguru.blogspot.com

http://professormsrao.blogspot.com

http://profmsr.blogspot.com

Charan, Ram (2007), *Leaders At All Levels: Deepening Your Talent Pool to Solve the Succession Crisis*, Jossey-Bass.

Covey, Stephen R. (1990), *The Seven Habits of Highly Effective People*, Free Press.

16

God is Making You Greater

> The heights by great men reached and kept were not attained by sudden flight, but they, while their companions slept, were toiling upward through the night.—*Henry Wadsworth Longfellow*

Do You Believe in Luck?

When I was doing a workout in gymnasium, a young man approached me and asked a question, "Dear Professor! People often say 'do your duty but don't look for rewards'. Don't you think it is a contradictory statement as we work only for rewards? Could you explain?" I smiled and said as follows:

I complimented for asking a good question and probably many youth may have this query in their minds. Lord Krishna said, "Action is the duty reward is not thy concern." That means man has to put in his efforts consistently without focusing too much on results as focusing too much on results diverts his mind from putting in efforts. Man gets discouraged when encountered with failures as he is more concerned about results than efforts. Besides, for some people success comes early, and for some people success comes late. Hence, our duty as human beings is to put in efforts regularly without getting unduly worried about success. When I explained in this way the young man smiled and said, "Thank you Professor for clearing my long unanswered query."

People often talk about 'luck' when someone achieves something. They ignore the hard work put in by the successful individual. The truth is that there are two forces that govern any individual. First is internal force, and second is external force. Man has to put in his best efforts to achieve the desired goals and objectives. However, the external forces often hinder in achieving success. When external forces favor, man can reach his tipping point. The external force is nothing but 'luck'. However, if you don't work hard and achieve success due to the favorable so-called external forces such as 'luck', your success will not last long enough. Hence, keep doing your best without looking for results and returns, and, over a period of time success will touch your toes. Here is a caution! The higher you achieve, higher the humility you must possess otherwise the success doesn't have any meaning.

God is Great

> If one advances confidently in the direction of his dreams, and endeavors to live the life which he has imagined, he will meet with success unexpected in common hours.—*Henry David Thoreau*

During my three decades of experience in varied capacities, I have seen a number of people living in their comfort zones and sailing smoothly. They take pride in playing safe in their lives, and often blame the people who failed in their lives. When the unsuccessful people bounce back from failures and make it big the critics regret for not having tried and, at times, they express envy over the success of others. In fact, when you sail smoothly you must know that you are not using your full potential. You can unlock your full potential only when you explore, fail, invent, and bounce back from failures with tenacity.

When you sail smoothly your inner potential lies hidden. However, when you face a severe storm you come out of your comfort zone, and start thinking in various ways and means to sail the ship smoothly to the shore and, you unlock your hidden potential ultimately. History reveals that the people who became great are the ones who faced several challenges in their lifetimes, not the ones who led cozy and comfortable lives. These great people rarely realized their inner strength and potential until they confronted with challenges. Hence, when you are confronted with challenges, God must be helping you discover your hidden strength, and is trying to get the best in you. Remember that whenever you face challenges in life, God has bigger plans for you, and you are destined to soar greater heights of success. God is great!

Hold Your Hope High

> Whenever you make a mistake or get knocked down by life, don't look back at it too long. Mistakes are life's way of teaching you. Your capacity for occasional blunders is inseparable from your capacity to reach your goals. No one wins them all, and your failures, when they happen, are just part of your growth. Shake off your blunders. How will you know your limits without an occasional failure? Never quit. Your turn will come.—*Og Mandino*

There is growing uncertainty everywhere. We can't predict what happens next. When we look at the problems of middle aged people especially, they continuously struggle to meet the needs of their children. Currently, children have higher expectations and aspirations from parents and society. Parents are not in a position to meet their expectations and they are constantly on toes to find out the ways to generate incomes. Similarly, companies find it tough to meet the rising expectations of customers and clients. With the rapid growth in technology, the expectations of the people are also rising rapidly. Hence, it has become a huge challenge for all of us.

It is said that a child looks at the future, the middle aged looks at the present, and the old aged looks back at the past. These are the stages for every person. Everyone has to experience this process, and there is meaning to life only when they undergo all these three stages. In the journey of life, everybody has challenges in family or finance or other challenges. It is true that people often fail in their lives. But they should not suspend their journey and must pursue up to the hilt as such failures are lessons providing human growth. Although it is easier to talk of failure and bouncing back, the process of bouncing back is indeed painful! Man should not lose his hope and confidence, and should strive towards success constantly.

REFERENCES

Author's Blogs:

http://professormsraoguru.blogspot.com

http://professormsrao.blogspot.com

http://profmsr.blogspot.com

PART IV
Coaching

17

Embrace and Facilitate Change Effectively

> Change can be exhausting when it's approached in the wrong way. Over my years of research, I've witnessed countless leaders try to implement change, but instead burn out their employees and create a sense of frustration in their organizations. This may seem like a classic case of what not to do, but this scenario is not unique to any kind of company, and it's growing more common as the rate of change accelerates.—*John P. Kotter*

People are often scared of change. When we are asked to change place of location, nature of work or in roles and responsibilities, and policies and procedures, we get tense. However, when we talk of changing the clothes, the foods, and the lifestyles we get excited. Why is it so? Does it not sound contradictory? But it is a fact that people resist change. We will discuss change from the perspective of Dale Carnegie first.

Dale Carnegie and Change Management

> People support a world they help create; and support a process that helps them succeed.—*Dale Carnegie*

Dale Carnegie stated that people must overcome six kinds of fears. They are 'fear of criticism', 'fear of failure', 'fear of old age', 'fear of poverty', 'fear of ill-health', and finally 'fear of death'. In the context of change, it is the 'fear of failure' and 'fear of criticism' that are the obstacles for embracing change.

The people in the workplace are scared of embracing change as the results of change are unpredictable and they doubt about the capability and competency in effecting the change. At times the loss of authority, fear of losing job and fear of coming out of the comfort zone make the change process complicated.

In fact, the fear of change is worse than the real change. When the real change takes place, people gradually overcome their apprehensions provided there is a strong and visionary leadership to facilitate the change process.

Everyone talks about change, and everyone knows that change pays off well. Everyone admits that change is the only thing constant in the world. Yet, people resist change. Is it because change is painful and stressful? The fact is that change is always helpful. If there were no change, the mankind would have remained in Stone Age only. Therefore, let us mentally prepare to shed the old outdated practices and procedures and wed new ones that lead to all-round peace and prosperity. Benjamin Disraeli rightly quoted, "Change is inevitable in a progressive society. Change is constant."

Treat Change as a Friend, not as a Foe

> A change leader looks for change, knows how to find the right changes and knows how to make them effective both outside the organization and inside it.—*Peter F. Drucker*

Some treat 'change' as a challenge, some as learning and some as an obstacle. Everything is there in your mind. You can treat 'change' as an opportunity to learn. You can treat it as an opportunity to grow. There is need for right attitude towards 'change' in today's world. And also there is need to develop an attitude to treat change as a friend rather than a foe.

The river that goes to sea undergoes several flows in different directions during the course of its journey and sometimes with slow and swift pace. So is the case of human life. Throughout human life, man undergoes several challenges such as peaks, valleys, smooth and rough terrains. The only successful people are the ones who accept and mould themselves as per the changing environment. Truth is that change is inevitable. Change is the mantra for your survival and success. The business scenario is changing rapidly and the organizations need to keep pace with it to reinvent and evolve accordingly.

Leaders and Change

Leaders find it tough to manage and effect change. Leaders are aware that change is the only thing constant in this world. They are proactive and treat change as a friend rather than a foe. They are aware that change is the key to organizational survival and growth.

Jack Welch cautioned, "If the rate of change on the outside exceeds the rate of change on the inside, the end is near." The only things constant in the corporate world are change, and competition. Every change is made for a reason. Nobody can survive without change. Change requires a new mindset, tool set, and skill set.

Unsuccessful Leaders and Change

> What the caterpillar calls the end of the world, the master calls a butterfly.—*Richard Bach*

Successful people often resist change while the unsuccessful people prefer to change as the latter tend to think in multiple ways to achieve success. Unsuccessful people are also aware that success comes at a cost. When we look at a leader like Abraham Lincoln, he was unsuccessful number of times. He made the world sit up and take notice during his tenure as the President of America by preserving the unity of America and ending slavery. He learned the lessons in a hard way during his initial failures. He knew what did not work to reach to the top and that helped him become one of the best Presidents of America. Similarly, when we look at Edison he was unsuccessful number of times in inventing bulb. But he made it possible as he knew what did not work. John Seely Brown, Xerox Corp's former chief scientist, rightly noted, "The more success you achieve—either as an individual or as an organization—the more difficult it is to change. All of the learning that led to one kind of success becomes implicitly coded and works against your ability to unlearn."

Facilitate Change

> We are not creatures of circumstances, we are the creators of circumstance.—*Disraeli*

It is a fact that organizations that create change can move more rapidly than the ones that manage change. And creating change is possible only when there is cooperation on the part of the organizational members to create change constructively. Leaders can change the fate of their organizations with the stroke of a pen. Hence, they must learn to use their pens to create rather than to manage change with the changing times and technologies for ensuring organizational excellence and effectiveness.

REFERENCES

Author's Blogs:

http://professormsraoguru.blogspot.com

http://professormsrao.blogspot.com

http://profmsr.blogspot.com

18

Marshall Goldsmith—A Coaching Legend

> When successful people write down goals, announce these goals to respected colleagues and involve the colleagues in helping them improve (in a supportive way), positive measurable change is much more likely to occur.—*Marshall Goldsmith*

Marshall's Book—What Got You Here Won't Get You There

When I was asked to conduct a workshop for senior executives of a prestigious global company on Dr. Marshall Goldsmith's book, *What Got You Here Won't Get You There* I felt excited as he had written foreword for my book titled *Soft Skills Enhancing Employabilty* and also for my son—Ramakrishna Sayee's book titled, *Script Your Success Story*. I personally admire Dr. Marshall Goldsmith for his humility to respond to my all mails. Although Marshall is a very busy man, he takes time to reply to my mails. Therefore, I thought it is a privilege to share about this humble global leadership guru and also about his book, and his lessons to people. I quickly glanced through the book and decided to share with my readers as well.

There are several lessons you can learn from his book, *What Got You Here Won't Get You There How Successful People Become Even More Successful*. The book is divided into four sections: The Trouble with Success, The Twenty Habits That Hold You Back from the Top, How We can Change for the Better, and Pulling Out the Stops. It contains total 15 chapters providing valuable takeaways to readers. Here are the takeaways in a nutshell:

People often take their success for granted. Those who reached top positions think that the strategies that worked in the past to reach to the top positions will work again to reach further higher positions. It is a myth as the needs, aspirations and expectations of the clients and customers are changing rapidly with the changing times and technologies. Hence, those who reached to successful positions must be careful and should not take their success for granted. They need to constantly learn and upgrade themselves, and change their ways and means to reach further higher positions.

The book unfolds that people are often obsessed with their past strategies to reach success and don't adopt new things leading to stagnation and preventing further career growth. Marshall says that there are 20 habits that become barriers for their further growth. People must identify these barriers and overcome to reach their next higher level.

Competition gets stiffer and tougher once the executives reach into senior leadership positions. Almost all senior executives are intelligent, smart working, charismatic, but very few reach to the CEO level. What differentiates senior executives from CEOs? At times it is the thin line that separates highly successful and just successful executives. The book helps the successful senior executives to cross the thin line and become more successful paving the way for CEO positions. To reach the tipping point in your corporate ladder you need to equip certain tools and techniques you find in this book.

The book helps you realize your shortcomings to reach senior leadership positions. It makes you humble. Marshall advises you to take feedback as feedback is the breakfast of champions. He counsels to listen carefully to others, apologize if you have made any mistakes, and follow-up thoroughly. Most of the senior executives may be aware of certain things written in this book. However, they still lack certain tools that Marshall provides and enlightens them to read and succeed in their senior leadership positions. The book is a good read for ambitious executives who like to reach senior positions quickly. Here is the profile of this legend:

Dr. Marshall Goldsmith—A Coaching Legend

Marshall Goldsmith

Dr. Marshall Goldsmith is a specialist in executive coaching. He is the *New York Times* and million copy best-selling author of *MOJO* and *What Got You Here Won't Get You There*. He is the number one coaching guru, and the seventh ranked management guru in the world as per the *Thinkers 50*. He is an executive coach who helps successful leaders become better by bringing out behavioral changes.

There are specializations in coaching. For instance, late C.K. Prahald was specialist in strategy related coaching and Richard Leiter is specialist in life coaching. However, Marshall is specialized in interpersonal skills and behavioral skills.

It is true that behind the success of every leader there is someone who laid the ladder for his or her growth. That ladder is none other than the executive coach in corporate world who constantly grills, grinds and makes leaders sharper and wiser through coaching and constructive feedback.

Coaches are the ladders who keep the ladders on the right side of the wall. Leaders know how to climb and why to climb but it is the coaches who know where these leaders should climb. It is said that behind the success of every man there is a woman. That is a traditional cliché. However, in the corporate world behind the success of every leader there is a coach who placed the ladder of the leader on the right side of the wall. Marshall has put the ladders of several leaders of Fortune 500 companies on the right side of the wall thus ensuring their success.

Few cynics opine that coaching is a management fad. Coaching is going to survive and play a crucial role in the corporate world. Although the term coaching is new, it exists since time immemorial. Due to the growing complexities in the corporate world, there is growing emphasis on coaching to enhance performance of leaders.

Marshall—A Level 5 Leader

According to Jim Collins, the level 5 leaders don't mind who gets credit. Their main job is to deliver the goods well without looking for any rewards. Besides, the level 5 leaders have the humility and professional will. Marshall Goldsmith is a Level 5 Leader in the language of Jim Collins who shaped several CEO's careers without taking credit. He is humble at core, down-to-earth, and is a thorough professional who means business.

Next to Peter F. Drucker, it is the Marshall Goldsmith who deserves Nobel Prize for his contribution towards management and executive coaching. He is a man with humility who is ready to handhold leaders beyond geographical boundaries. He has great global appeal with a huge fan base. Norwegian Committee must constitute Nobel Prize for the management discipline, and must award Nobel Prize to this leadership legend.

REFERENCES

Author's Blogs:

http://professormsraoguru.blogspot.com

http://professormsrao.blogspot.com

http://profmsr.blogspot.com

19

Coaching and Talent Conversations

As leaders shift their focus to customers and quality, they realize that the old authoritarian leadership style does not work anymore. To achieve quality, service, and rapid response, leaders must utilize all available talent. They must find ways to inspire, involve, and empower employees. They must create a work environment that encourages commitment, innovation, and cooperation. Instead of evaluating, leaders now coach. Instead of doing, they delegate. Instead of telling, they facilitate. No one is expected to boss anyone. Everyone is expected to participate.—*Dr. Suzanne Willis Zoglio*

The term 'Talent Conversations' sounds strange right! It has been highlighted by Roland Smith and Michael Campbell, who authored the book titled, *Talent Conversations: What They Are, Why They're Crucial, and How To Do Them Right.*

Talent conversations is a subset of talent management. It is the process wherein the superiors have a dialogue with their subordinates by handholding, motivating and grooming them as leaders and managers and also by imparting various skills, abilities and knowledge. It is also known as touch time as superiors stay in touch with their subordinates by investing their precious time to raise the spark among their employees and develop them as competent professionals. It helps employees grow well, and deliver goods effectively within the organization.

Importance of Talent Conversations

Talent conversations help connect superiors with subordinates in the workplace quickly. It is the need of the hour as these days most of the bosses talk about performance and results rather than guiding their subordinates. Hence, emphasizing on the career growth of employees, though Talent Conversations builds bridges between superiors and subordinates, and it ultimately paves the way for organizational excellence and effectiveness. Nowadays, employees prefer to work with supervisors and leaders who handhold them, guide them, and groom them as leaders.

Talent Conversations is a win-win for both superiors and subordinates as superiors not only earn respect but also get the tasks executed successfully from their subordinates, and subordinates can also grow quickly in their careers by working with such superiors.

Current Scenario

It is unfortunate that most of the entrepreneurs are presently more interested in generating business and less interested in developing their talent. There are some companies who grew in terms of generating their revenues but failed to nurture their precious human resources thus hitting the rock bottom later. Therefore, the leaders, entrepreneurs and supervisors must focus on Talent Conversations to encourage their talent and retain the same for their organizational excellence and effectiveness. It helps in building the leadership pipeline and encourages employee engagement, and employee loyalty towards the organization.

Talent Conversations is an integral part of coaching and leadership development. Especially, coaches can make use of this tool to tap the hidden potential among the coaches and nurture the same thus bringing behavioral changes and enhancing performance. Hence, companies must engage passionate coaches to nurture the talent. To conclude, Talent Conversations is an amazing tool to develop the talent within your organization and build the leaders around you. Hence, use this tool effectively to achieve greater organizational success. Remember the words of Benjamin Disraeli, "The greatest good you can do for another is not just share your riches, but to reveal to him, his own."

REFERENCES

Author's Blogs:

http://professormsraoguru.blogspot.com

http://professormsrao.blogspot.com

http://profmsr.blogspot.com

Smith, Roland and Campbell, Michael (2011), *Talent Conversations: What They Are, Why They're Crucial, and How To Do Them Right*, Center for Creative Leadership.

20

What Got You Here Will Get You There

> Successful people will almost always respond constructively to advice and input when they are involved in selecting the behaviors and selecting the advisors. By making the process confidential (not identifying raters), people will tend to focus on what they need to improve, not who did the rating. It is hard to deny the validity of items that we say are important as evaluated by raters that we respect!—*Marshall Goldsmith*

Hire a Great Coach to Become a Great Leader

Coaches are the ladders for leaders. They know how to place the ladders on the right side of the wall. Leaders have vision and the coaches fine-tune their vision with a practical touch. Coaches align the energies and efforts of busy leaders through their passion, wisdom and experience. Coaches are aware that what worked for these leaders to reach the present position won't work in future to scale further corporate heights. And it is their job to enlighten and educate the leaders to reach further higher positions through their coaching and direction. Coaches help leaders realize their hidden potential. They help leaders reach their maximum capabilities. Bob Nardelli, CEO of Home Depot believes that without a coach, people "will NEVER reach their maximum capabilities."

There is a thin line that separates the senior leaders from leaders and CEOs from non-CEOs, and it is the coaches who know that thin line and make sure that the good leaders deliver effectively to become great leaders. That thin line is nothing but a different mindset that is needed to reach further higher positions. Precisely, coaches help good leaders become great leaders. Although most of the leaders are aware of this thin line, they may not be able to focus to cross over due to their busy schedules and pressures. It is the coaches who would handhold good leaders to become great leaders. It is the coaches who uncork the hidden potential among the leaders to become great leaders. It is the coaches who allay hidden phobias and apprehensions of leaders. It is the coaches who make everything possible as they are cut out for such roles and responsibilities.

Hence, dear good leaders! Don't waste your precious time by brooding over too much. Take time off from your busy schedules and ruminate for a while. Hire a great coach to excel as great leaders as what got here won't get you there without a great coach.

What Got You Here Will Get You There

> Executive coaches are not for the meek. They're for people who value unambiguous feedback. All coaches have one thing in common; it's that they are ruthlessly results-oriented.—*Fast Company Magazine*

You must be surprised with the title of this sub-heading in this chapter as basically the title would have been *What Got You Here Won't Get You There How Successful People Become Even More Successful* authored by Marshall Goldsmith. Marshall rightly said that people often get complacent with their success and positions and take everything for granted resulting in stagnation in their careers. In fact, what worked to reach to the current position might not work to reach further higher positions.

With the rapid growth in technology, the expectations and aspirations of the customers are changing rapidly. And most of the times it becomes tough to predict customers' expectations. Hence, leaders must regularly know the pulse of customers and evolve their business strategies accordingly. At the same time they must also constantly hone their leadership skills and abilities as per the changing needs. It is the coaches who can guide and groom these leaders with their research, consultancy and corporate experience. They have their own strategies and being good at core areas they keep close eye on the latest developments in the domain and enlighten the same to the leaders. Since leaders are so busy with their hectic schedules, they may not find time to focus on their career growth. Hence, hiring professional coaches paves the way for their quick career growth. These leaders reap rich rewards out of coaching by paying peanuts to coaches. The returns out of coaching are amazing indeed!

Survey by The Hay Group, International shows, "Between 25 percent and 40 percent of Fortune 500 companies use executive coaches." It is obvious from this survey that companies are gradually realizing the importance of hiring coaches for grooming their leaders. There are a number of coaches with credentials whom the top CEOs and companies hire and benefit. Then why don't you hire and scale the corporate ladder quickly by hiring professional coaches? Remember always: *What Got You Here Will Get You There* only when you hire great coaches.

REFERENCES

Author's Blogs:

http://professormsraoguru.blogspot.com

http://professormsrao.blogspot.com

http://profmsr.blogspot.com

PART V
Leadership

21

Leadership is not a Passing Cloud

Leadership is not a popularity contest. It is taking responsibility.—*Professor M.S. Rao*

Leadership is not a Hype, but a Hope

A leader is a dealer in hope.—*Napoleon Bonaparte*

When a participant asked me in one of my leadership training programs why too much of hype was being created on leadership globally I thanked the participant and responded as follows:

If you search in Google with terms, 'leader' and 'leadership' you get around half a billion hits. It indicates the kind of interest these terms are creating globally. People are very much fascinated about 'leadership' and 'leaders', and are eager to know what makes people excel as great leaders. It appears like a lot of hype. But the truth is that the terms deserve great attention as it provides hope for the mankind especially for the depressed and dejected.

The world is facing unprecedented crisis due to the changes in technology. The changes are too rapid and people find it tough to cope up with it. The present global corporate world is ridden with several scandals and corruption. The politics are ridden with foul play without any ethics. At times, people breakup their relations for silly reasons. To prevent people from getting cynic and pessimistic, we need leaders who can take responsibility, walk their talk, and lift the morale of the people through their vision, direction, influence and example. Hence, leadership is certainly a hope, not hype as it provides a ray of hope for the people who grope in darkness, who don't know what to do, and who hit lows in their lives. Dr. Martin Luther King, Jr. rightly remarked, "We must accept finite disappointment, but never lose infinite hope."

Leadership is not a Passing Cloud

Leadership depends on the longevity of the leader. If you look at leaders like Abraham Lincoln, Mahatma Gandhi, Winston Churchill, and Martin Luther King Jr, to name a few, they are great leaders remembered even today. They have left indelible impression in minds of the people, and are remembered beyond their generations. Popularity of these leaders is intact whether their time was good or bad because of the trust, goodwill, and respect they enjoyed among the people.

There are many leaders who come and go, and whose popularity is like a passing cloud. However, there are exceptional leaders who are beyond popularity and time, and are remembered forever. These leaders are undeterred by temporary downfalls as they are true leaders born for the people, and they not only remain in the minds of the people but also in the hearts of the people.

To ensure leadership longevity, leaders must constantly innovate and reinvent, find out what people want, and serve them with a sincere heart. Above all, they must be continuous learners and take feedback constantly.

Remember that real leaders remain in the hearts of the people irrespective of generation as they never crave for popularity but crave for making a difference in the lives of others. John Bytheway rightly put it: "It is better to be respected then it is to be popular. Popularity ends on yearbook day, but respect lasts forever."

Are Good People Good Leaders?

> Effective leadership is not about making speeches or being liked; leadership is defined by results not attributes.—*Peter Drucker*

Good leaders may not be good for all people and good people may not be good leaders. The statement sounds strange, right! Leadership is a blend of both bouquets and brickbats. It involves taking the responsibility, walking the talk, influencing others, and making tough decisions when the situation demands. A good person may be in the good books of all but may not possess leadership potential. The good people who want to excel as leaders must realize this bitter truth before undertaking their leadership journey. There are leaders who are basically considered good by many people but when they delivered goods as leaders they invited criticism thus becoming bad for few people. At the same time there are people who were considered neither good nor bad initially but proved well through their leadership qualities and excelled as good leaders. Hence, when you want to become a leader remember this truth and decide whether you want to become a leader. And, remember one thing: being good is a bonus and an asset but it doesn't guarantee you the leadership success.

There were instances where good people turned out to be ineffective leaders as they wanted to please everybody. Remember what Sun Tzu said, "Leadership is a matter of intelligence, trustworthiness, humaneness, courage, and discipline.... Reliance on intelligence alone results in rebelliousness. Exercise of humaneness alone results in weakness. Fixation on trust results in folly. Dependence on the strength of courage results in violence. Excessive discipline and sternness in command result in cruelty. When one has all five virtues together, each appropriate to its function, then one can be a leader." To summarize, all good people may not be good leaders but all good leaders may be good people.

Avoid Leadership Decay

> Leadership and learning are indispensable to each other.—*John F. Kennedy*

Are you hardwired with your old successful leadership practices and principles? Do you think you can succeed with your old leadership tools and techniques? Then you are trapped into leadership decay. It is time to know leadership decay to prevent yourself from decaying.

Leadership decay is about context and situation. People often think that what worked them to be successful previously will be relevant to achieve further success in future. In the prevailing rapid changing world, what worked in a particular scenario may not work in other scenarios. For instance, Jack Welch himself admitted that his management styles don't work in the current context as there are rapid changes in technology. He said, "The Jack Welch of the future cannot be like me. I spent my entire career in the United States. The next head of General Electric will be somebody who spent time in Bombay, in Hong Kong, in Buenos Aires. We have to send our best and brightest overseas and made sure they have the training that will allow them to be the global leaders who will make GE flourish in the future." In addition, Marshall Goldsmith substantiated the same in his famous book—*What Got You Here Won't Get You There: How Successful People Become Even More Successful*. It means the leaders who reached to the current position may not reach to the next higher positions if they don't change their leadership tools and techniques, and secrets and strategies because what worked for them to reach to the present success will not work to reach their next level. He says, people often think and apply the old practices as they were successful in the past thus decaying their leadership.

Leadership decay starts the movement the leaders get into the trap with their old mindset and practices. Hence, leaders must realize it, and overcome successfully to stay ahead of others. Leaders must continuously listen to their people to avoid leadership decay. They must continuously learn, and take feedback to enhance leadership effectiveness. Above all, they must learn to change, and reinvent constantly with latest technological tools and techniques to remain relevant, and to succeed in this cut-throat competitive world.

REFERENCES

Author's Blogs:

http://professormsraoguru.blogspot.com

http://professormsrao.blogspot.com

http://profmsr.blogspot.com

22

Level 6 Leaders

> All of the great leaders have had one characteristic in common: it was the willingness to confront unequivocally the major anxiety of their people in their time. This, and not much else, is the essence of leadership.—*John Kenneth Galbraith*

According to Jim Collins, there are five levels of leadership. The level 1 leaders are good at their work individually. They can contribute their best individually both efficiently and effectively. The level 2 leaders are not only efficient and effective but also work in teams effectively thus gelling well with team members. The level 3 leaders are competent managers who can get the work done effectively and efficiently from level 1 and level 2 leaders. The level 4 leaders think ahead of level 3 leaders as they have clear vision to where they intend to go and take their team members forward. Finally, the level 5 leaders are highly passionate and don't mind who get credit for their contribution. They have personal humility and professional will. Such leaders take organizations to greater heights of glory. Level 5 leaders are required to take organizations from good to great. Are there level 6 leaders beyond level 5 leaders? Let us explore it.

Level 6 Leaders

> No person can be a great leader unless he takes genuine joy in the successes of those under him.—*W.H. Auden*

Level 6 leaders work with passion, patience and perseverance. They emphasize on values and ethics. They empathize with others. They believe in values based leadership. They build further leaders thus ensuring longevity of the organizations. They know how to inspire the people. They are master trainers and mentor others. They are transformational leaders with passion to make others believe in themselves for the good of others. They are knowledge leaders with specialized knowledge. They are thought leaders who see the invisible and forecast the future requirements that are beyond the reach of normal leaders.

Level 6 leaders strive for the personal and professional success of their followers. They handhold, guide and groom them as leaders. They create more leaders to take things forward. They ensure the longevity of the organization without expecting any rewards and returns.

To summarize, level 6 leaders create more leaders. They are above level 5 leaders. They are humane and kindhearted. They believe in soft leadership that blends both soft and hard skills. These leaders are legends who will be remembered for several generations for their commitment and making a difference in the lives of others.

Nobel Prize for Management Discipline

> The number one difference between a Nobel prize winner and others is not IQ or work ethic, but that they ask bigger questions.—*Peter F. Drucker*

Nobel Prize is regarded as the most prestigious award in the world for contributions to the fields of physics, chemistry, medicine, literature, peace and economics. It has been named after Alfred Nobel from Sweden, who came out with 355 inventions including dynamite. He wrote in his will that his entire wealth would be utilized for the people who contribute mankind in the areas of physics, chemistry, peace, medicine and literature. The prizes are given to living individuals who contributed enormously in their areas. At the time of categorizing, management as a discipline was not included as it was evolving as a science. Perhaps that is the reason why there is no Nobel Prize in the category of management.

Mahatma Gandhi was nominated for Nobel Prize for Peace but was not awarded. Subsequently, the Norwegian Nobel Committee regretted for not giving him prize. Likewise deserving leaders like Eleanor Roosevelt, Václav Havel, Ken Saro-Wiwa, Sari Nusseibeh and Corazon Aquino were not awarded.

Peter F. Drucker who hated to be called "guru" wrote 31 books and advised stalwarts like Jack Welch, Jim Collins, Stephen R. Covey, Ken Blanchard and Warren Bennis. His books have been translated into more than 20 languages. He was a simple and humble person at core. He coined the concept of Management by Objectives (MBO) and predicted the rise of knowledge workers. He left a better place to live for others. It is said, "There isn't any Nobel Prize in management thinking and writing. But it's just as well—because it would have been won every year by the same man—Peter Drucker." We have many such gurus and leaders in management discipline. Hence, members of the Norwegian Nobel Committee must consider including management and mathematics as disciplines and declare Prizes annually as a mark of respect to the champions of these disciplines.

REFERENCES

Author's Blogs:

http://professormsraoguru.blogspot.com

http://professormsrao.blogspot.com

http://profmsr.blogspot.com

23

Growing Indian Management Gurus Globally

> If a gathering of crows is a murder, a group of foxes is a skulk and there is also a flight of butterflies, a descent of woodpeckers and many, many more, what should we call a collection of management gurus? And the answer is—An orchard of gurus.—*www.thinkers50.com*

When I received mail with the final list of management gurus from thinkers 50, I was overwhelmed to find the listing of a few relatively young management thinkers. The entry of young gurus in the list excited me and changed my perception that there can be young management gurus as well. Usually, there is a general perception that the top management thinkers are highly experienced and fall in the bracket of Baby Boomers. However, the 2011 list of Thinkers 50 debunked the myth that age is not a deterrent to achieve global management guru status.

What is Thinkers 50?

The Thinkers 50 ranks the most important living management thinkers alive today. Stuart Crainer authored a book titled, *The Thinkers 50: The World's Most Influential Business Writers and Leaders*. It periodically conducts voting of various global thought leaders based on certain parameters who contributed to the management field. The thought leaders could be educators, economists, authors, executives, consultants, social scientists, and scholars.

People who voted showed interest towards younger lot sending Baby boomers Stephen Covey from 29 to 47 and Tom Peters from 19 to 24 positions. However, there is senior lot whose rank rose up such as Vijay Govindarajan from 24 to 3, Marshall Goldsmith 14 to 7, Dave Ulrich from 31 to 23 to name a few. The list also indicates mushrooming Indian management thinkers such as Nitin Nohria (Ranked 13), Dean of Harvard Business School, Nirmalya Kumar, Pankaj Ghemawat, Vineet Nayar, Rakesh Khurana, Sheena Iyengar, and Subir Chowdhury.

Previously, four Indians found place in the list heading C.K. Prahalad in number one position, Ram Charan at No. 22, Viay Govindarajan at No. 23, and Rakesh Khurana at No. 45. It is exciting to note that in the current list the number of Indian management thinkers have doubled. They are making their presence felt. They are being accepted globally and recognized for their contributions to management. However, it is unfortunate that Ram Charan is missing from the list.

Guru Criteria

The criteria for management gurus' status are that their presence as gurus and impact of their ideas across the world, presence on the academia and corporate world, and charisma with international exposure and visibility. Their research background, any exclusive contribution to the domain of management and, above all, the number of Google hits indicates their popularity. The guru must ideally blend either academic or industry background with extraordinary contribution towards management field through research and innovation. Those who crave for international attention must slog hard with a passion to make a difference to society and that catapults them to the top. For instance, Vijay Govindarajan's innovation and his concept of 'Housing for Poor @ $300' put him on the international map. Remember that it is always the cream that comes to the top. The list changes every time with the entry of new gurus who contribute unique research in the area of management.

The Thinkers 50 must also come out with lifetime achievement for one living Management Guru every time. I am sure it inspires others and contributes to the cause of management as there is no Nobel Prize for management discipline.

Challenges for Gurus

The gurus should not take their rankings for granted. They must learn and grow continuously with humility. They must become more responsible to deliver their services to make a difference in the lives of others. Above all, they must pave the way for other upcoming gurus graciously before being pushed away by next generation gurus.

Indians' Appetite for Management

The list clearly reveals the growing number of Indian management gurus who shone after crossing the seas. We cannot find any Indian working currently in India excelling as guru except Vineet Nayar who has been ranked 40. Probably, one of the reasons is that the gurus have better research facilities, academic ambience, exposure, network and plenty of opportunities without any prejudices in overseas. In addition, most of them work in prestigious global business schools. Hence, if the same conditions prevail in Indian business schools, we can find more Indian management gurus growing from Indian soil as well. Government must realize that there is a huge potential among Indian management faculty but lacking certain infrastructural and research facilities. If the same is provided, we can find more Indian management gurus growing from Indian business schools and Indian soil than in an alien soil.

The list also shows the growing appetite among Indian management thinkers as global management gurus through their research and contributions. When you look at Vijay Govindarajan who is popularly called VG globally, he is specialized in innovation. His three box approach written along with Chris Trimble is very popular and published in *Harvard Business Review* titled, "The CEO's Role in Business Model Reinvention" urging forward-looking CEOs to manage reinvention with a "three-box approach". This approach emphasizes on managing the present (box! 1), selectively forgetting the past (box! 2), and creating the future (box! 3). Leaders need to operate in all three boxes simultaneously to achieve the desired organizational outcomes.

Nitin Nohria made all Indians proud by becoming the first Indian to head as the dean of prestigious Harvard Business School. VG also made Indians proud through his contribution in the area of innovation and standing in 3rd place as a management guru. Other Indians such as Nirmalya Kumar, Pankaj Ghemawat, Vineet Nayar, Rakesh Khurana, and Subir Chowdhury have equally made all Indians proud through their contributions.

Studies reveal that most of the top business schools in the world have faculty members from Indian origin. It shows the strength of Indians and their acceptance globally in the area of management. Previously, it was in science and technology and currently it is into management, Indians are doing well. There is a huge demand for quality Indian management faculty members globally who are a blend of industry, research, teaching, training and consultancy background so that they can effectively integrate all these areas to excel as successful faculty members.

Indian vs. International Ambience

There is a perception to take Indians living in India for granted. In addition, there are too many politics within Indian academic institutions. At times cream is prevented from rising to the top. Of course, it rises ultimately! However, egalitarianism and meritocracy prevails in advanced countries especially in a country like America. They respect knowledge of the people, not the origin of the people. They don't see whether rich or poor or white or black. They only see competencies, not color. They see only strengths, not skin. They see skills, not status. Likewise, there are number of ways they are ahead of us, and these are some of the reasons why Indian management thinkers go abroad and grow as gurus.

Indians in Alien Environment

Leaving Vineet Nayar who grew within India, most of the gurus grew in an alien land. In fact, alien environment especially advanced countries is highly competitive. It is a kind of "perform or perish", "do or die", "swim or sink". Indians often perform amazingly well, do effectively, and swim and sail successfully in overseas shores.

Indians have great heart and are always jubilant with the success of their compatriots beyond the borders. Not only as management gurus but also there are number of Indians who rose in other sectors such as Indra Nooyi, Arun Sarin and Vikram Pandit to name a few. Most of the time the Indian thinkers going abroad are constantly in their effective zones and that brings out best in them. They also collaborate leaving competitive spirit and that pays them immensely. Similarly, there are a number of reasons that make global Indians stand out. As it has been evidenced from Thinkers 50, Indian management faculties have huge potential to grow as management gurus both locally and globally provided there is favorable academic ambience and equal opportunities for them. Let us salute these living management legends for making India proud both locally and globally.

> I shall pass this way but once. Therefore any good that I can do, or any kindness that I can show, let me do it now for I shall not pass this way again.—*William Penn*

REFERENCES

Author's Blogs:

http://professormsraoguru.blogspot.com

http://professormsrao.blogspot.com

http://profmsr.blogspot.com

www.thinkers50.com

24

Appreciate Others and Excel as a Leader

> We are at the very beginning of time for the human race. It is not unreasonable that we grapple with problems. But there are tens of thousands of years in the future. Our responsibility is to do what we can, learn what we can, improve the solutions, and pass them on.—*Richard P. Feynman*

Face Problems Squarely

In India, people often blame politicians for all the problems. In fact, politicians are the biggest scapegoats in democracy as they cannot talk against people for fear of losing their votes during elections. Politicians often present smiling faces despite being criticized by people. People have so many expectations and they know that it is impossible for them to accomplish. They take solace by blaming politicians. People make several mistakes and ultimately they pin responsibility on politicians.

People must know that politicians have come from people only. People must know the slogan that people get the government they deserve. Next time when you blame politicians blame yourself first as you have elected such politicians. Next time when you pin responsibility on politicians think yourself first how much responsible you are.

John C. Maxwell says in his book *Be All You Can Be*, "We have developed a society in which people would rather take the easy way out; we have become a relief-syndrome culture. This type of society does not make good leadership training ground. But those who are willing to pay the price will make it, and the world will sit back and wonder how these successful men and women ever got so lucky. Luck has nothing to do with it; they were simply willing to do what all the rest of the people were unwilling to do."

You cannot expect a problem-free society. Problems will be there as long as people are there. If people don't have any problems, they will be in their graveyards. Hence, let us not blame politicians for all the problems we face. We must take responsibility, and learn to face the problems squarely so that we can grow stronger and wiser and pass on a better society to our next generation.

Great Minds with Small Hearts is a Greater Challenge

> If you are doing big things, you attract big men. If you are doing the little things, you attract little men. Little men usually cause trouble.—*Winston Churchill*

The problem with some people is that they have great minds but with small hearts. They cannot digest when their competitors make it big. They express their envy, and at times, play politics to pull down the legs of their competitors. Developing great mind alone is not enough to become a great person. What is needed is to develop both great mind and great heart with an attitude of gratitude to make a difference. Of course, it requires ample of attitudinal adjustment and fine-tuning.

I have come across with many people who are intelligent with great ideas. I often get fascinated with their ideas and insights. But I find a few of them having small hearts thus defeating the very purpose of having great mind.

We need a society that is full of great minds with great hearts which makes people great and our society great. We need people with honesty and integrity, and with simplicity and humility. When we have such great people we can find peace and prosperity everywhere.

See Positive Things in Others to Excel as a Leader

> The longer I live, the more I realize the impact of attitude on life. Attitude to me is more important than facts.... We cannot change our past...we cannot change the fact that people will act in a certain way. We cannot change the inevitable. The only thing we can do is play on the string we have, and that is our attitude. I am convinced that life is 10 percent what happens to me and 90 percent how I react to it. And so it is with you...we are in charge of our attitudes.—*Charles R. Swindoll*

Do you see positive things in a negative person? Do you remember positive people rather than negative people in your mind? Do you remember sweet memories rather than sweat memories? Do you emphasize on ideas rather than on issues and individuals? If the answer to these questions is "yes" then you are a true leader who can handhold others. You can throw the light and show the way for others.

Most of the people blame their circumstances and people around them for their failures. They often think that they are only right and others are wrong. They think that they are the victims of circumstances. They hardly have any internal locus of control. Such people cannot grow as leadership material. Here are the tips to view positive things among others to grow as a successful leader:

- Avoid pessimism. Develop optimism.
- Learn to look at things positively.
- Develop the attitude of gratitude.
- Let go off the past. Learn to look at things on a clean slate by avoiding negative perceptions against individuals.
- Focus on your goals to fill your mind with energy and enthusiasm.
- Enjoy the nature.
- Go to a serene place and spend your time to allow positive thoughts to enter your mind.
- Above all, make a difference in the lives of others.

When you follow these tips you will develop positive attitude towards life and the people around you. You will give your best and you get the best, and excel as a true leader.

> Those who educate children well are more to be honored than they who produce them; for these only gave them life, those the art of living well.—*Aristotle*

REFERENCES

Author's Blogs:

http://professormsraoguru.blogspot.com

http://professormsrao.blogspot.com

http://profmsr.blogspot.com

Maxwell, John (2007), *Be All You Can Be: A Challenge to Stretch Your God Given Potential*, David C. Cook.

Epilogue

> If I am walking with two other men, each of them will serve as my teacher. I will pick out the good points of the one and imitate them and the bad points of the other and correct them in myself.—*Confucius*

I have authored this book to underscore and elevate the role of educators who are the real leaders in the society. I have dwelt on academic leadership, management education, success, coaching and leadership with anecdotes, illustrations, case studies, and short stories to help you excel as leaders. If this book helps you achieve your expectations, it will have done its job. If you put this book down feeling that you are better equipped with adequate teaching tools and techniques to achieve your academic excellence and leadership, I feel that my work as an author has been accomplished.

I would appreciate your valuable feedback to make improvements to this book. You may post your feedback at http://speakerwiki.org/speakers/Professor_MSRao or send me an email: profmsr7@gmail.com. If you want information on the seminars and workshops on leadership that I conduct or my availability as a speaker for your group or conference, please contact me. You may also visit my Blogs http://profmsr.blogspot.com, http://professormsrao.blogspot.com, and http://professormsraoguru.blogspot.com which are widely read globally. These blogs pertain to Learning, Leadership, Coaching and Soft Skills. Please post your comments directly on the blogs themselves, as it helps others appreciate your ideas. If you find the blogs interesting, please share the links with your friends, as knowledge grows when shared.

You may share your thoughts about *Soup for Academic Leaders: Acquire Teaching Tools to Achieve Your Academic Leadership Success* on Facebook, Twitter, and the websites you visit. You can also blog about it or write a book review.

I pray for your success.

Professor M.S. Rao

Founder, MSR Leadership Consultants India

Bibliography

Leaders At All Levels by Ram Charan

The Seven Habits of Highly Effective People by Stephen R Covey

Talent Conversations: What They Are, Why They're Crucial, and How To Do Them Right by Roland Smith and Michael Campbell

Be All You Can Be by John C. Maxwell

Online References

Author's Blog: http://profmsr.blogspot.com

Author's Blog: http://professormsraoguru.blogspot.com

Author's Blog: http://professormsrao.blogspot.com

http://members.shaw.ca/mdde615/tchstyles.htm

www.fiu.edu/~pelaeznm/images/Resource/Martha/EEX%204601%20 Instructor's%20Notes/Unit_1_EDP3218.ppt

http://en.wikipedia.org/wiki/Classroom_management

http://www.usingenglish.com/forum/teaching-english/54168-good-teacher-like-candle-consumes-itself-light-way-others-3.html

https://www.acsi.org/webfiles/webitems/attachments/002072_Classroom %20Management.ppt

http://books.google.co.in/books?id=s5S3ixTQw3YC&pg=PA28&lpg =PA28&dq=%C2%B7%

www.chench.com/quotes/teachers-and-teaching-children

http://www.yourdictionary.com/cue-card

http://www.answers.com/topic/cue-card

http://www.wisegeek.com/what-is-a-teleprompter.htm

http://www.forbes.com/2007/09/22/india-happiness-survey-face-cx_rd_0921autofacescan02.html

http://en.wikipedia.org/wiki/Peter_Drucker

www.thinkers50.com

http://www.ntlf.com/html/lib/faq/ts-indiana.htm